The Modern Language Association of America

Approaches to Teaching
Masterpieces of World Literature

Joseph Gibaldi, Series Editor

Approaches to Teaching Ibsen's *A Doll House*

Edited by

Yvonne Shafer

The Modern Language Association of America   1985

Copyright © 1985 by The Modern Language Association of America

Library of Congress Cataloging in Publication Data

Main entry under title:

Approaches to teaching Ibsen's A doll house.

  (Approaches to teaching masterpieces of world literature; 7)
  Bibliography: p.
  Includes index.
  1. Ibsen, Henrik, 1828–1906. Dukkehjem—Addresses, essays, lectures. 2. Ibsen, Henrik, 1828–1906—Study and teaching—Addresses, essays, lectures. I. Shafer, Yvonne, 1936–   . II. Series.
PT8861.A77 1985   839.8′226   85-2989
ISBN 0-87352-487-X
ISBN 0-87352-488-8 (pbk.)

Cover illustration of the paperback edition: *Two People (The Lonely Ones)* (1895), drypoint engraving, by Edvard Munch.

Published by The Modern Language Association of America
Astor Place, New York, New York

CONTENTS

PREFACE TO THE SERIES

In *The Art of Teaching* Gilbert Highet wrote, "Bad teaching wastes a great deal of effort, and spoils many lives which might have been full of energy and happiness." All too many teachers have failed in their work, Highet argued, simply "because they have not thought about it." We hope that the Approaches to Teaching Masterpieces of World Literature series, sponsored by the Modern Language Association's Committee on Teaching and Related Professional Activities, will not only improve the craft—as well as the art—of teaching but also encourage serious and continuing discussion of the aims and methods of teaching literature.

The principal objective of the series is to collect within each volume a number of points of view on teaching a specific work of world literature, a literary tradition, or a writer widely taught at the undergraduate level. Preparation begins with a wide-ranging survey of instructors, which enables us to include in the volume the philosophies and approaches, thoughts and methods of scores of experienced teachers. The result is a sourcebook of material, information, and ideas on teaching the subject to undergraduates.

The series is intended to serve nonspecialists as well as specialists, inexperienced as well as experienced teachers, graduate students who wish to learn effective ways of teaching as well as senior professors who wish to compare their own approaches with the approaches of colleagues in other schools. Of course, no volume in the series can ever substitute for erudition, intelligence, creativity, and sensitivity in teaching. We hope merely that each book will point readers in useful directions; at most each will offer only a first step in the long journey to successful teaching. We may perhaps adopt as keynote for the series Alfred North Whitehead's observation in *The Aims of Education* that a liberal education "proceeds by imparting a knowledge of the masterpieces of thought, of imaginative literature, and of art."

Joseph Gibaldi
Series Editor

PREFACE TO THE VOLUME

Henrik Ibsen's play *A Doll House* is an appropriate choice for the first modern dramatic classic to be considered in the Modern Language Association's Approaches to Teaching Masterpieces of World Literature series. Ibsen is often called "the father of modern drama," and *A Doll House* is frequently taught as the first play in modern drama courses. A source of great excitement when it was first published and performed, it continues to hold a place on the stage, in collections of plays, and in the classroom.

The articles in this volume are designed to assist teachers at all levels but primarily at the undergraduate level. Included are discussions of material that will be familiar to experienced Ibsen scholars but that will be new to teachers beginning their careers or teaching *A Doll House* for the first time. There is material that will be of use to the Ibsen scholar and to the teacher who wishes to expand an already considerable acquaintance with Ibsen and his plays. It is also hoped that instructors will consider encouraging graduate students to use the volume.

In the introduction I discuss current Ibsen scholarship and current attitudes toward Ibsen and toward teaching *A Doll House*. We are in a very good period for Ibsen: there are rich and varied critical reappraisals, new and vital translations, and more frequent productions than in the recent past. This positive state is reflected in the body of the volume. Part 1, "Materials," includes a survey of editions of *A Doll House*; a comparative evaluation of translations, by Thomas Van Laan; and a discussion of suggested and required readings for students, aids to teaching (films, recordings, etc.), and essential reference works, background studies, and critical studies.

Part 2, "Approaches," contains fourteen essays by scholars who teach *A Doll House* in courses ranging from the freshman to the graduate level, in different types of colleges and universities throughout the United States. An appendix listing participants in the survey of Ibsen instructors, a list of works cited, and an index conclude the book.

I am grateful for the assistance given by contributors and survey participants alike. I would particularly like to note the help of the members of the Ibsen Society of America, including Irving Deer and Thomas Van Laan, who served as readers for the initial proposal and made valuable suggestions, and Richard Hornby, who read material, commented on plans for the volume, and gave encouragement throughout the preparation. I would like to call attention to the determination of another member, Brian Johnston, who completed a first and second draft of his essay while teaching temporarily in Beirut during the hostilities there. Thomas Shafer gave me some very helpful suggestions after reading the book in draft form. Throughout the project, I have profited from the advice and prompt assistance of the series editor, Joseph Gibaldi. Finally, I am very grateful for the suggestions and encouragement given by the two manuscript readers, Einar Haugen and Elaine H. Baruch, and the sympathetic assistance given to me by Otto Reinert and Carla Waal.

Yvonne Shafer

INTRODUCTION: TEACHING ALL OF *A DOLL HOUSE*

The publication of *A Doll House* by Henrik Ibsen on 4 December 1879 has been noted as a major event in the development of dramatic literature. The play was first presented in Stockholm by the Royal Theatre on 8 January 1880. Within the month productions followed in Christiania (now Oslo) and Bergen. Next came productions in Germany, including the famous one with a "happy ending" furnished by Ibsen for the star, Hedwig Niemann-Raabe, who stated that *she* would never leave her children. Both the published play and the productions caused excitement and controversy. Nora's departure made an impact throughout society: it was, in the now famous phrase, "the door slam heard around the world." Today an instructor teaching *A Doll House* faces the challenge of recreating the vividness, commitment, and true passion that Ibsen conveyed in his play. With every classic comes a burden of unquestioned, often outdated criticism and unexamined attitudes that veil the work from the reader. In teaching *A Doll House* we cannot obviate the influence of more than one hundred years of often misguided criticism and often ineffectual or altered productions. Nevertheless, the instructor who is determined to teach the play in all its dimensions can cut through much of the scholarly dust that sometimes seems to cover Ibsen's works.

Like most important writers, Ibsen has passed through various stages of acceptance and rejection. In his lifetime he was perceived by many people as a *folkefiende*—an enemy of the people, a man whose dangerous plays (particularly *A Doll House*) undermined society. In the anxious response to the plays' perceived ideas, the stunning artistic achievements of Ibsen's dramaturgy were often ignored. By the beginning of the twentieth century, the structural techniques that Ibsen introduced had been imitated by second- and third-rate writers, and he seemed not so much the "father" as the "grandfather" of modern drama. For the first half of this century Ibsen was seen as out-of-date, passé. As Eva Le Gallienne remarked, "Critics used to talk a lot about 'the old museum piece . . . moth-eaten old something,'" and Le Gallienne was thought to be rather odd, still championing those old, dour plays ("Acting" 16). Nevertheless, audiences flocked to see the plays when Minnie Maddern Fiske, Eleanore Duse, Le Gallienne, and others performed them. The first notable American production of *A Doll House*, however, in 1883, was a failure: it starred the Polish actress Madame Modjeska and had a happy ending. Fiske was quite successful in 1894, creating a sensation because of her realistic acting technique and the content of the play. Her pioneering work in Ibsen roles led a number of actresses to perform Nora, including Ethel Barrymore (with her brother John as Dr. Rank), in 1905; Alla Nazimova in the twenties and thirties; and Ruth Gordon, in a 1937 adaptation by Thornton Wilder.

Around mid-century the critical reaction toward Ibsen changed. M. C. Bradbrook's *Ibsen the Norwegian: A Revaluation* (1946) was a turning point, and since that book open and deep admiration for the plays has replaced the condescension of earlier critics. By 1962 F. L. Lucas could write, "To decry Ibsen as out of date is—out of date" (130).

Recent decades have proved a stimulating and rich period for both the study and production of Ibsen's plays. The 150th anniversary of Ibsen's birth in 1978 stimulated many international tributes. Pratt Institute and the Mellon Programs in the Humanities supported the five-day Ibsen Sesquicentennial Symposium in Brooklyn, which included presentations by the director Richard Schechner, the author Bernard Dukore, the critic Robert Brustein, the actress Stella Adler, the director Alan Schneider, the psychiatrist Rollo May, and the novelist Elizabeth Hardwick. On the final day of the celebration, the Ibsen Society of America was established, on the motion of the Ibsen scholar Einar Haugen, with Rolf Fjelde as president. The University of British Columbia in Vancouver celebrated the anniversary by holding a conference with the scholars Evert Sprinchorn, James Walter McFarlane, Michael Meyer, Martin Esslin, and others and the actress Janet Suzman. Both conferences featured speakers associated with the theater as well as with scholarship, and the title of the conference was "Ibsen and the Theatre."

1979 witnessed many events commemorating the centennial of the publication of *A Doll House* and many productions of the play in professional theaters and in colleges and universities.

In 1983, in Pittsburgh, the American Ibsen Theatre presented its first season with a highly praised production of *A Doll House*, directed by Travis Preston, with Marina Coblentz as Nora. Today the lively state of Ibsen production, the critical reappraisals of his work, and the availability of modern, colloquial translations afford us an unprecedented opportunity to study and appreciate Ibsen's *A Doll House* both on the stage and in print. The challenge for the instructor teaching the play is to bring the literary and the theatrical dimensions together.

One way to achieve this objective is to become aware of the multiple interpretations of *A Doll House* that are available in productions and in libraries. Many readers tend to view realistic plays such as those by Ibsen in his middle phase as one-level, unambiguous thesis plays. This tendency creates several problems in criticism and in teaching. First, seeing *A Doll House* and *Ghosts*, among others, as merely thesis plays leads to a dismissal of the plays as passé because of changes in society. (In 1928 Brecht stated that the use of new drugs to cure syphilis made *Ghosts* obsolete!) Second, the assumption that the plays are straightforward statements about social problems leads to a one-dimensional interpretation of character: Nora is a heroine and her husband a villain; Dr. Stockmann in *An Enemy of the People* is a wholly admirable hero; Mrs. Alving in *Ghosts* is a heroine and Pastor Manders a prig. Such interpretations do a disservice to Ibsen and ignore the many levels of action, parallel structures, and complexities of theme and symbolism; they render complex individuals, acting in difficult situations, as stick figures playing stereotyped roles in a purely black-and-white picture of society. Teachers of *A Doll House* need to lead students beyond the readily understandable story and the character of Nora to an appreciation of the whole play.

A *Doll House* presents students with no serious problem of literal comprehension: there are no unfamiliar terms and no confusing political intrigues. The issue of "relevance" that is so vexing in discussions of some classics does not arise here. The problem, in fact, is in the opposite direction: students want to discuss the play in direct relation to their views of our society, and while the discussions can be very lively and exciting (one instructor remarks, "I have to caution my students to maintain civilized behavior"), many of the riches of Ibsen's work may be lost or ignored. A narrow interpretation, from whatever point of view, diminishes the play. As Michael Meyer notes,

> It is the tragedy of books carrying a particular message for their times that they tend to be remembered for the wrong reasons. *A Doll's House* and its successor, *Ghosts*, are particular examples; critics still occasionally write about *A Doll's House* as though it were a play about the hoary problem of women's rights—an attitude largely conditioned by the habit, among British and American critics, of consulting Bernard Shaw's *Quintessence of Ibsenism*, that brilliantly misleading book which should have been called *The Quintessence of Shavianism*, before writing about any Ibsen play. *A Doll's House* is no more about women's rights than Shakespeare's *Richard II* is about the divine right of kings, or *Ghosts* is about syphilis, or *An Enemy of the People* is about public hygiene.   (*Ibsen: A Biography* 457)

What the play is about is certainly one question that students may profitably explore. Most recent criticism suggests that it is about many things and that it is not a clearcut thesis play at all. The essays in part 2 of this volume discuss many different interpretations and approaches. Excellent recent criticism enables the instructor to help students appreciate Ibsen's achievement in the structure of the play as a whole as well as the play's theatrical effectiveness and rich use of metaphor, symbolism, irony, double entendre, outright comedy, and repetition of words and phrases.

Ibsen's language deserves special consideration. The first productions of his plays in English were handicapped by wooden, bowdlerized translations—some of which are still in use today. Michael Meyer has a good deal of fun quoting some of the lines from the first translation of *A Doll's House*:

> HELMER.   You are first of all a wife and mother.
> NORA.   . . . I believe that I am first of all a man, I as well as you—
> or at all events, that I am to try to become a man.   (*Ibsen: A Biography*
> 460)

Fortunately, instructors have a wide choice of translations now and should compare available editions. A detailed discussion of editions and a separate discussion of translations by Thomas Van Laan are in part 1. But a few thoughts on the importance of the translation and on the attitudes of instructors are appropriate here.

To begin with, the translation of the title itself is controversial. The play achieved fame and notoriety under what became its traditional title, *A Doll's House*. Today a number of scholars, directors, and actors prefer the title *A Doll House*, which was first used by Rolf Fjelde. Discussing his translation of the play, Fjelde stated,

> There is certainly no sound justification for perpetuating the awkward and blindly traditional misnomer of *A Doll's House*: the house is not Nora's, as the possessive implies; the familiar children's toy is called a doll house; and one can make a reasonable supposition that Ibsen, intending an ironic modern contrast to the heroic ring of the house of Atreus or Cadmus, at least partially includes Torvald with Nora in the original title *Et dukkehjem*, for the two of them at the play's opening are still posing like the little marzipan bride and groom atop the wedding cake. (*Ibsen: Four Major Plays* xxxvi)

As the reader will see, some of the contributors to this volume agree with Fjelde, while others prefer the traditional title.

Many of the participants in the survey of instructors indicated a strong preference for one particular translation, which they chose for its theatrical quality, for the American or British idiom, and for the colloquialism of the speech. Yet many are unaware of problems with the translations they are using, indifferent to the merits of various translations, or not even cognizant of the translation in their selected edition. Thomas Van Laan's comparison of translations provides an antidote to that neglect.

Survey respondents also indicated the various ways in which they find pleasure in teaching the play: some find it ideal for introducing students to modern drama, some find its controversial aspects effective for engaging students in discussion, and most find the play's themes exciting and significant and enjoy bringing out its theatrical qualities, often through performance in class. But a few instructors find no joy in Ibsen and still see him as the "old museum piece." Instead of filling in the questionnaire, one respondent wrote a letter questioning the value of the play:

> I find the play, like much of Ibsen's work, terribly dated, and I would only include it in a course where its historical significance could be emphasized. I believe it is fashionable to include ADH in the so-called women's lit courses, yet even in this context I am not sure it is appropriate. . . . Although Nora grows somewhat, she matures only to the point where she can walk away from her problem.

This letter undoubtedly represents the views of other instructors queried who did not take the time to respond. I hope material in this volume will remove doubts regarding the value of *A Doll House*. In studying and teaching the play for many years, I have found that the better one knows it, the more one admires it for its characterization, thematic development, language, and structure. It is a play that will only be appreciated when examined in depth. Fortunately there is a growing awareness of the need for such analysis in introducing students to the full power of Ibsen's *A Doll House*.

Part One

MATERIALS

Yvonne Shafer

Editions and Translations

Many editions and translations of *A Doll House* are in use in American colleges and universities. Some selections are made after careful consideration of those available by an individual instructor, some represent a compromise among numerous instructors in different sections of the same course, and some are arrived at rather haphazardly. Because cost is a factor, paperback editions are more popular than hardcovers. Some instructors have strong preferences. The choice is complicated by the many types of courses in which the play is taught, including specialized Ibsen courses, women's studies courses, directing and acting courses, play analysis, and survey courses in literature and composition. The following sections discuss the most widely used editions and translations and give reasons for their use in various courses.

Collections of Ibsen Plays

The instructor able to read and teach Ibsen's plays in the original language may consult the standard Norwegian edition in twenty volumes that was published in Ibsen's lifetime (*Samlede Vaerker*, 1898). *Et dukkehjem* is in volume 6 of this edition. Unfortunately, the edition is not in many American libraries, but a three-volume edition with modernized spelling is available in paperback (*Samlede Verker*, 1960).

Instructors who use translations and teach the work in courses that include more than one Ibsen drama generally choose a collection of Ibsen plays, several of which are available in both paperback and hardcover. The collection that has moved strongly to the fore in recent years is Rolf Fjelde, *Ibsen: Four Major Plays*. Many instructors indicate that they have chosen this anthology because "it reads well and plays well" and is "the most modern and fluent." The work is also popular because of its very low cost. Several respondents mention the value of Fjelde's foreword and his choice of the other plays in the volume (*The Wild Duck*, *Hedda Gabler*, and *The Master Builder*). Instructors teaching seminars in Ibsen often choose Fjelde's *Ibsen: The Complete Major Prose Plays*, which is a more expensive hardcover book.

After Fjelde, Eva Le Gallienne's *Six Plays by Henrik Ibsen* or *Eight Plays by Henrik Ibsen* are most frequently used. In addition to *A Doll's House*, the former contains *Ghosts*, *An Enemy of the People*, *Rosmersholm*, *Hedda Gabler*, and *The Master Builder*; the latter also includes *The Wild Duck* and *The Lady from the Sea*. Le Gallienne contributed greatly to the popularity of Ibsen in this country, and her translations were important in presenting theatrically effective versions in a popular edition with an excellent introduction. Unfortunately, many who teach *A Doll House* using these collections do not seem to be aware of the omission of a critical segment in the scene

3

between Nora and Dr. Rank. An instructor who realized this fact after using one of the editions for several years writes, "I was dismayed to find the Eva Le Gallienne Modern Library translation is expurgated." One respondent knows about the deletion and uses the edition in combination with another translation of the complete play. Instructors indicate that they use Le Gallienne's collections because of the stageworthiness of the translations and because of the variety of the Ibsen plays in the volumes.

Other anthologies of Ibsen plays include Michael Meyer's translations in his two-volume *Ibsen: Plays* and Ghosts *and Three Other Plays*; *Four Great Plays by Ibsen*, with translations by R. Farquharson Sharp (referred to as the "Bantam edition"); *Four Major Plays*, translated by James Walter McFarlane and Jens Arup; and A Doll's House *and Other Plays*, translated by Peter Watts (referred to as the "Penguin edition").

Meyer's second volume of *Ibsen Plays* contains *A Doll's House*, *An Enemy of the People*, and *Hedda Gabler*. In addition to *Ghosts* his 1962 collection includes *A Doll's House*, *An Enemy of the People*, and *Rosmersholm*. Like the other editions under discussion, these collections are inexpensive. Instructors who use the collections are enthusiastic about the notes that precede each of the plays, but some instructors in the United States feel the translations of Meyer, Watts, and McFarlane, which use a British idiom, create a barrier to students' appreciation. (Notably, several Canadian instructors prefer these editions *because* of the idiom.) One respondent comments, "I have recently switched from the Meyer translation to the Fjelde because the latter seems less formal (perhaps I mean more American) and at the same time, more in keeping with the theatre values of the play." Another says, "I prefer American English to British English." An instructor who does not object to the British idiom praises Meyer for using "contemporary diction without losing Ibsen's quality and intent."

The popularity of the Bantam edition of *Four Great Plays* continues despite the British idiom and the old-fashioned diction. (For example, Nora speaks of hiding the Christmas tree until it is "dressed.") Some instructors mention the good, but rather brief, introduction by John Gassner, but most seem to select the edition because of price. Included in the collection are *A Doll's House*, *Ghosts*, *An Enemy of the People*, and *The Wild Duck*. Except for a seven-page introduction, there is no material to assist the student, whereas the other editions mentioned (which, in fact, are about the same price or even cheaper) have the advantages of a recent translation, chronologies, introductory material, and, in the Fjelde, a selected bibliography. Despite James Walter McFarlane's influence as a critic and translator and the widespread use of his *Oxford Ibsen* for background material, his paperback edition (including *A Doll's House*, *Ghosts*, *Hedda Gabler*, and *The Master Builder*) is infrequently used in this country. The collection is interesting because it contains, in addition to his notes, the alternate ending to *A Doll House*, which Ibsen wrote for a production in Germany. The Penguin edition is used by a few instructors and, like the Bantam edition, is chosen chiefly for its price. It contains *A Doll's House*, *The League of Youth*, and *The Lady from the Sea*.

Anthologies Containing the Works of Several Authors

Many instructors teach *A Doll House* in courses that involve several other literary works. Often the choice of text is made by a committee of teachers. Many instructors, however, have a marked preference for a particular anthology. A very popular one is *Literature and the Human Experience*, edited by Richard Abcarian and Marvin Klotz, which contains Otto Reinert's translation of the play. One instructor says she likes the volume because of the "international scope of the selections," the discussion of three critical approaches to literature, and the excellent glossary of literary terms. Another instructor writes, "I like the selections of short stories, poems, and the other plays. Also the text is arranged thematically." Another praises the edition for the afterwords to each selection, which "pack a great deal of helpful material into a small space."

The Reinert translation of Ibsen's play is also found in *The Heath Introduction to Literature*, edited by Alice S. Landy, as well as in Otto Reinert and Peter Arnott, *Twenty-Three Plays*, which is used by a number of instructors. One wrote that he selected this edition because it contains "the greatest number of good modern plays for the price." A smaller anthology is Reinert and Arnott, *Thirteen Plays*, which is used in a number of classes and which contains "a good cross section of plays." Several instructors remark on the pleasing colloquial quality of the translation. Another popular anthology for use in courses covering several genres is *Literature: An Introduction to Fiction, Poetry, and Drama*, edited by X. J. Kennedy. It contains the Fjelde translation and is liked for its interesting content and "workable approach to literature and literary terms." All the anthologies mentioned are relatively inexpensive paperbacks.

In conclusion, it may be said that although cost is certainly an important factor, instructors can readily find reasonably priced collections that contain good translations of the play as well as useful teaching material. Interestingly, respondents to the survey indicate a desire for even better texts; the ideal anthology containing *A Doll House* would include a good modern translation, essential critical material, a comprehensive introduction, a chronology, an extended bibliography, and photographs of productions of the play.

English Translations of *A Doll House*

Thomas F. Van Laan

What one reads in translation is, you know, always in danger of being more or less misunderstood; for translators are unfortunately all too often lacking in understanding. (Henrik Ibsen, 11 April 1898)

These remarks, which Ibsen uttered at a banquet in his honor held by the Swedish Society of Authors in Stockholm, constitute his version of the familiar Italian proverb *Traduttore: traditore* (translator: traitor). Ibsen's English translators readily quote other, less potentially incriminating comments by Ibsen on translation, but not these, and Michael Meyer does not even include them in his account of this talk in his biography of Ibsen. The translators no doubt feel that the context lessens the significance of these remarks—Ibsen is urging that Swedes, Danes, and Norwegians make the slight effort required to read one another's works in the original—but both the remarks and the context clearly show Ibsen's fear that translation is likely to constitute betrayal. This is a fear that Ibsen has shared with a good many other major writers, and it is certainly understandable in an artist who spent many months on every play and went through numerous revisions striving to make every word, every turn of phrase, every sound, and every rhythm exactly right—that is, to make each a carefully chosen and precise contribution to the overall design of the play. The result of such careful artistry is that no English version of an Ibsen play could be a truly faithful "carrying over" of the original, unless Ibsen had been like Beckett, at home in both languages and pretty much his own translator.

To compound the difficulty, many of the English versions that reach the stage are not even translations, because theater people prefer using something called an "adaptation." This is a text composed by someone with numerous writing credits in theater, movies, and television who is ignorant of the play's original language and must use a "literal" crib prepared by someone else who knows the language but evidently lacks the intelligence to create a genuine translation; sometimes an existing genuine translation is used without authorization or acknowledgment. Theater people prefer an adaptation because it gives them another familiar name to include in the advertising, and—more important—it helps free them from the demands imposed by the dramatist so that they may more unrestrainedly indulge their own "creativity." Adapters feel little responsibility to the text of the original. They alter it to make it more readily available for the audience to whom they are catering, and they do whatever they can to make up for the "artistic shortcomings" of the original author—in other words, they condescend to

6

both their authors and their audiences. Adaptation is probably the best technique for transferring a mere entertainment from one language to another, but there is no excuse for it when the work to be transferred is by a writer of Ibsen's stature. The result is necessarily a greatly diluted and distorted remote echo of the original, and its only justification is that it gives employment to minor dramatists.

Although many people who think they have seen *A Doll House* actually haven't, the picture is not quite so bleak as I have painted it thus far. Fortunately for English-speaking readers without a command of Dano-Norwegian (the vast majority of them), there exist a number of English translations of Ibsen that compare favorably with the best that translation can do. They follow the original speech by speech and line by line and evidently seek to convey (in Rolf Fjelde's words) "the text, the whole text, and nothing but the text" (*Ibsen: Four Major Plays* 1: xxxiv). They are not Ibsen pure, but some of them often come close to conveying Ibsen as well as he can be conveyed once another language and another consciousness have intervened.

Not all translations are of equal quality, however, and the English-speaking reader should select a translation with care. The purpose of the following pages is to provide some guidance in this process. After a much too brief attempt to indicate what all translations of *A Doll House* fail to carry over— apparently necessarily—I then turn to the main function of these pages, a comparative evaluation of six of the translations of *A Doll House* that the English-speaking reader is most likely to come in contact with, because of their availability in anthologies and inexpensive paperback editions and, in one case, because of its inclusion in what is generally recognized as the "standard" edition of Ibsen in English. The six translators and the editions I have used are William Archer, Eva Le Gallienne (*Six Plays*), James Walter McFarlane (*Oxford Ibsen*), Rolf Fjelde (*Ibsen: The Complete Major Prose Plays*), Michael Meyer (*Ibsen: Plays*), and Otto Reinert (*Twenty-three Plays*). (I had also intended to include the translation by R. Farquharson Sharp, because it appears in the Bantam edition, *Four Great Plays by Henrik Ibsen*, but a little research soon revealed what the publishers neglect to mention, that Sharp's translation was first published in 1910 in the Everyman Library edition. Translations have a way of aging, and I decided that one version of that vintage—the important one by Archer—was sufficient.)

The aspects of the original that all these translations fail to convey—or to convey adequately—are of two sorts. The first consists of local and incidental details, indicative of Norwegian culture, for which there seem to be no English equivalents. Most significant for English-speaking readers is the loss of numerous details reflecting the Norwegian fondness for personal titles that categorize an individual according to profession and exact status within a profession and thereby place her or him within a carefully calibrated social hierarchy. Since it is the hierarchy, not Torvald alone, that suppresses Nora and against which she rebels at the end of the play, this loss is of no little consequence. Such losses could be somewhat reduced—for readers, at least— if translators would revive a practice that seems, for no easily discernible reason, to have fallen out of favor: the explanatory footnote.

Footnotes would not help much, however, in making up for the other source of failure these translations have in common, their failure to render not just particular details but a central component of the dramatic design. The *vidunderlige* (variously translated as "the wonderful," "the wonderful thing," "the miracle," and "something miraculous") that Nora awaits half hopefully and half fearfully is but the most prominent and explicit detail of an extensive, continuously recurring motif dramatizing the assumption of Nora's society and of the people who constitute it that they should view themselves as "blessed" regardless of their circumstances. One's lot, according to this motif, is not the result of one's efforts, nor is it consonant with one's desert. It is given to one from outside, given by God, and in response, whatever that lot may be, one must be content, even thankful. This extremely important component of the play's design is virtually the only indication that Nora revolts not merely against her husband and the society whose agent he is but also, and perhaps finally more importantly, even against the heavens as that society conceives them.

In addition to these failures, all the translations are to some extent adaptations. Errors are prevalent enough to be worth mentioning, and each of the translators has one or more limitations that interfere with reproducing the original text with whatever precision a different language will allow. Fortunately, none of these translators could even come close to the sort of disastrous mess perpetrated by the first translator of the play into "English," a Danish schoolteacher named T. Weber, whose "specimens of unconscious humor" are sampled by Michael Meyer in his biography of Ibsen (460–61) and include the following exchange:

> NORA.   As I am now, I am no wife for you.
> HELMER.   I have power to grow another.

But errors there are, both flat mistranslations and distortions that lose some important sense of the original. Meyer himself is capable of such a howler as having Krogstad, in act 1, assure Nora that what she did "is no bigger nor worse a crime than the one I once committed," when he obviously should be saying, as he does in the original, that the crime *he* "once committed" and thereby ruined his "whole social position" was "no bigger nor worse" than hers. Such mistranslations should be readily discoverable, however (though Meyer's version was supposedly performed before it was published), and therefore it is far more dismaying to find distortions like Nora's "[there's] something I'd love to say to Torvald" (also Meyer), when the original ("there's something I have such an enormous desire to say so that Torvald could hear it") clearly signifies the urge to perform an act of deliberate rebellion; or, in McFarlane, Nora's saying, as Torvald is about to get Krogstad's letter, "Yes, I'm very tired. I just want to fall straight off to sleep," when the original's "nu vil jeg snart sove" more probably means "now I will soon sleep," an apparently deliberate double entendre on Nora's part. All the English versions contain some mistranslations (though none of the others is as serious as the one from Meyer cited above), and all contain numerous distortions. The champion for errors among the six is Eva Le Gallienne, whose deviations from the text even include two significant omissions: the second paragraph of the opening stage direction, which is necessary to make sense of a good deal of the dialogue that follows, and—one hopes it is an error—the wonderful moment in the second act consisting of ten speeches and part of another, during which Nora shows Rank the stockings of her costume and teases him about his response.

Three of the translators share a characteristic of language that, while not involving errors, is necessarily a limitation from the point of view of American spectators and readers. William Archer, McFarlane, and Meyer are British, and, as is to be expected, their versions are full of words and phrases like "porter" (where Fjelde uses "delivery boy"), "quarter" (for "three months"), "made ducks and drakes of them," "nanny," "one endless slog," "mayn't," "on Boxing Day," "gay subaltern life," "drawing room," and "oh, hullo." This is no limitation at all for British spectators and readers, of course, and even most Americans will have little difficulty understanding most of these expressions; nonetheless, their frequency is sufficient to cast the play in a somewhat unfamiliar idiom and therefore slightly distance it. It remains a bit foreign, as if it hadn't been entirely translated. As might be imagined, Archer's version is the most British—as well as sounding faintly archaic. Of the three British translators Meyer is the most free of British expressions, but he is capable of producing both "drawing room" and "oh, hullo" in the space of four brief speeches.

Archer's version has problems that are more serious than its Britishness and its archaic flavor, and only publishers interested solely in saving money would nowadays select it for reprinting. Critics reject Archer's translations as dated and as stiff and awkward, especially in the scarcity of contractions resulting from Archer's too rigid adherence to the original, which naturally does not employ contractions according to English patterns. Oddly enough, however, the translation's worst flaw stems from a failure to follow the original closely enough. Archer evidently had no ear for the rhythms of speech, for he constantly eliminates repetitions and otherwise reduces what the characters say to such an extent that although the information carries over the attitudes of the characters and their verbal identities—their speech prints— do not. Ibsen's Nora asks Torvald why they can't begin to squander money a bit, since "Now, you know, you get a big salary and will be earning lots and lots of money," while Archer's Nora merely says, "You know you'll soon be earning heaps of money." Similarly, where Ibsen's Nora declares, "It is I who saved Torvald's life," Archer reduces the sentence to "I saved Torvald's life." What Archer loses in these examples is, respectively, Nora's delight and her pride. Sometimes he loses a great deal more, as in the case of Krogstad, whose peculiar style—his elaborately careful, overprecise, labored wordiness—virtually disappears from view. One sentence nicely illustrates this loss. Ibsen has Krogstad say, "You know, naturally, just as well as all the others, that I one time a few years ago happened to commit a thoughtless act." Archer renders it, "Of course you know, like every one else, that some years ago I—got into trouble." The circumlocutions, repetitions, and euphemisms of the original are not typical Norwegian but typical Krogstadese, his natural form of utterance, here exaggerated a trifle by his desire to sound innocent, as in the effort to put as many words as possible between "I" and "happened to commit."

Rolf Fjelde remarks that "it lies in the nature of the languages that an English translation will regularly run shorter and more concise than the text in Norwegian or Danish" (*Ibsen: Four Major Plays* 1: xxv); perhaps—but, as Fjelde's own translations show, certainly not to any great extent. Where the reduction is especially noticeable, as in Archer's version, it probably betrays the elimination of some locally significant or characteristic verbal rhythm. And there is no excuse for this, since Norwegian syntax is sufficiently similar to English that its rhythms can readily be translated. Archer consistently fails in this respect, in the early pages, no doubt, because he does not perceive the dramatic significance of the rhythms he reduces—surely he must have heard them!—later, perhaps, as much from carelessness, for, in a pattern not untypical of these translators, Archer's version becomes "freer"—less immediately responsive to Ibsen's text—as he goes along.

By far the worst of these translations is that by Eva Le Gallienne. Her rendering of Nora's first-act advice to Mrs. Linde, "It would be much better for you if you could go to a spa," as "What you need is a rest. Couldn't you go to some nice watering-place?" typifies the chief failures of her version, for "watering-place"—surely no longer in currency when Le Gallienne used it—is copied from Archer, and the rest of the passage is so loose and approximate that it begins to look more like vague paraphrase than translation. The copying from Archer is constant, and while it is most noticeable in verbatim rendering of his stage directions, especially as Le Gallienne gets further along in the text, there is also considerable borrowing of specific words and turns of phrase. The effect is disconcerting, suggesting that Le Gallienne felt insufficiently at home with the original or unsure of her ability to render her understanding of it in English. Judging from her constant deviations from the original when she wasn't copying Archer, one would have to conclude that the problem was indifference. The omission of exclamations—ranging from semiprofane outbursts like "å Gud, å Gud" and "herregud," through dismissive snorts like "pyt" and "å fy," to Tesmanlike verbal tics ("hvad")—suggests some intentional pattern, and since most of these omissions come in Nora's speeches and are accompanied by the substitution of "Father" for the original's "pappa," it looks as if she's trying to elevate Nora in some way. Most of her deviations reveal no clear purpose, however, and they become—like Archer's, though they far outnumber his—steadily more extensive as the text progresses. To illustrate them, I provide the following parallel passages from near the end of the play; the first passage is my literal rendering of Ibsen, the second comes from Le Gallienne's version:

Literal version:

HELMER.   I have the capacity to become a different person.
NORA.   Perhaps—if the doll is taken from you.
HELMER.   To be parted—to be parted from you! No, no, Nora, I can't grasp that thought.
NORA (*goes in to the right*).   The more surely it must happen. [Stage directions]
HELMER.   Nora, Nora, not now! Wait till tomorrow.
NORA (*putting on her cloak*).   I can't be spending the night in a strange man's rooms.
HELMER.   But can't we at any rate live here like brother and sister—

Le Gallienne version:

HELMER.   But if I were to change? Don't you think I'm capable of that?
NORA.   Perhaps—when you no longer have your doll to play with.
HELMER.   It's inconceivable! I *can't* part with you, Nora. I can't endure the thought.
NORA (*Going into room on the right*).   All the more reason it should happen. [Stage directions]
HELMER.   But not at once, Nora—not now! At least wait till tomorrow.
NORA (*Putting on cloak*).   I can't spend the night in a strange man's house.

> HELMER.   Couldn't we go on living here together? As brother and
> sister, if you like—as friends.

This kind of sloppiness may be owing to changes made during the rehearsals—for Le Gallienne performed her translations—but whatever the
reason, the text remains a long way from the original. It not only lacks
accuracy—of content, emotion, and rhythm—it also loses Ibsen's economy.

James McFarlane's *Oxford Ibsen*, which includes draft material, infor-
mative appendixes, and often illuminating introductions, is virtually
indispensable to English-speaking readers seeking to do serious study of
Ibsen. The translations themselves, however, if that of *A Doll House* is a
good example, leave something to be desired. McFarlane's version is almost
as relentlessly British as Archer's, and it also contains numerous unfelicitous
expressions, especially near the beginning. McFarlane seems to have difficulty with tricky passages, tending to cast them in clumsy and unlikely turns
of phrase, as when he has Torvald exclaim, "Here we go again, you and your
frivolous ideas!" and "Has it got the sulks, that little squirrel of mine?"
McFarlane also introduces such jarring expressions as "juvenile delinquents"
(when Torvald is instructing Nora about the disastrous consequences of
mendacious mothers) and "baby doll" (when Nora is talking about how her
father used to call her his "doll-child" or "doll-baby"). The translation's most
serious failing, however, is the fear of metaphor it tends to display. From
time to time Ibsen's characters reveal the habit of breaking forth with rather
self-consciously explicit metaphors that they then make even more conspicuous by deliberately extending them throughout a speech or conversation.
A primary example of this tendency is the imagery of shipwreck running
through the third-act dialogue between Krogstad and Mrs. Linde. The imagery is dramatically significant, for it enables the characters not only to
express their feelings but also to construct a joint verbal pattern to image
and anticipate the new life they will build together. McFarlane greatly
reduces the impact of this pattern by taming its individual components, as
when he changes "Look at me; now I'm a shipwrecked man on a broken
hulk" to "Look at me now: a broken man clinging to the wreck of his life"
and translates "Two shipwrecked people" as "two castaways." This evident
fear of metaphor also appears in McFarlane's rendering of one of Nora's
most telling speeches during her final scene with Helmer. When the original
Nora states, "This is a settlement, Torvald," she deliberately echoes and
appropriates his image of a few minutes earlier, "You're going to stay here
and render me an account." McFarlane's translation of Nora's line as "We
are going to have things out, Torvald" may catch the general idea, but it
wholly loses the particular dramatic point of Nora's actual words.

Michael Meyer's tendency to play down Ibsen's metaphors is almost as thorough as McFarlane's. By having Mrs. Linde say, "I'm in the same position as you," rather than the original's "I too am like a shipwrecked woman on a broken hulk," he avoids one repetition of the image; and he completely eliminates the financial metaphor from Torvald's and Nora's exchange by reducing their speeches to "You're going to stay here and explain yourself" and "You and I have got to face the facts, Torvald." A more serious and consistent limitation of Meyer's translation is the looseness with which he follows Ibsen's text; in this respect his translation resembles Le Gallienne's, though Meyer is less extreme. Like Le Gallienne he gets looser as he goes along. The example below comes from the end of act 2; my literal rendering of the original is followed by Meyer's version.

Literal version:

> HELMER (*takes her hands*).   Now, now, now; none of this alarmed wildness. Now be my own little lark, as you usually are.
>
> NORA.   Oh, yes, I'll be that, all right. But go on in for a while; and you too, Dr. Rank. Kristine, you must help me get my hair done up.
>
> RANK (*quietly, as they leave*).   There surely isn't something—something or other on the way?
>
> HELMER.   Oh, far from it, dear fellow; it's nothing at all but this childish anxiety I told you about.

Meyer version:

> HELMER (*takes her hands in his*).   Now, now, now. Don't get so excited. Where's my little songbird, the one I know?
>
> NORA.   All right. Go and sit down—and you, too, Dr. Rank. I'll be with you in a minute. Christine, you must help me put my hair up.
>
> RANK (*quietly, as they go*).   There's nothing wrong, is there? I mean, she isn't—er—expecting—?
>
> HELMER.   Good heavens no, my dear chap. She just gets scared like a child sometimes—I told you before.

Among other things, this looseness makes possible a sprinkling of French words and phrases: when in act 1 Rank enters to find Nora talking to Mrs. Linde, he fears he may "be *de trop* here too"; when Mrs. Linde leaves, Nora says, "*Au revoir*"; and when Rank has spoken too openly in act 2, he asks whether he perhaps "ought to say—*adieu*." This last seems scarcely an adequate translation of the original's "But perhaps I ought to go—forever," but my objection is less to the specific distortion than to the false tone the

French provides, as if Meyer were trying to locate the characters in some upper-class, well-educated, sophisticated social sphere. There may be people who talk this way, but Ibsen's characters don't, and I cannot believe that the social position the mannerism suggests is really appropriate.

Rolf Fjelde's translation displays some of the limitations characteristic of the other versions. There are occasional small omissions, such as the stage direction in which Torvald "takes her [i.e., Nora] by the chin"; and since Le Gallienne omits this stage direction too, Fjelde's dropping of it serves as one of several instances in which he seems to be following her version a bit too closely. Meyer's translation of Rank's delicate question about Nora's condition is far too explicit, but Fjelde's version—"There's nothing wrong— really wrong, is there?"—is *so* delicately expressed as to suggest that Fjelde has missed the point. Other occasional mistranslations occur—such as "You were all upstairs" for "you [singular form] were already upstairs" and "Both parts of it" for "Both the one and the other" (i.e., whatever is involved)— as well as several turns of phrase that do not quite capture the sense of the original: Nora would scarcely, for example, advise Mrs. Linde to go off to a "bathing resort." Fjelde also displays a touch of McFarlane's and Meyer's avoidance of conspicuous verbal effects, as is shown not only by his slight suppression of overt metaphor in a few speeches but even more definitely by his reluctance to follow Ibsen's characters in another typical verbal feature, their tendency to repeat certain key words. Although Ibsen's Nora, in the space of two brief speeches, speaks three times of the coming or not coming of "det vidunderlige," using the same two words each time—words often heard before this in the play, moreover—Fjelde gives us "the miraculous thing," "miracles," and "the miraculous event."

Otto Reinert's translation lacks this kind of elegant variation in reproducing Ibsen's repetitions of major key words; "det vidunderlige," for example, is consistently "the wonderful"—although English-speaking readers and spectators may not be able to accept an adjective where a noun ought to occur. Reinert also usually carries over Ibsen's metaphors, even though he too— like McFarlane and Meyer—eliminates Nora's pointed echo of Torvald's accounting metaphor (in Reinert's case, the echo is lost because Torvald's line is reduced to "You'll stay here and answer me"). Reinert is also to be commended for his efforts—far greater than those of the others—to capture some of the details indicative of Norwegian culture (he even includes a couple of explanatory footnotes), and, best of all, despite a few minor errors, he almost always renders correctly the gist of a passage. This is not to say, however, that Reinert's translation is free of defects. Although he is consistent in his repetitions of major key words, Reinert is not nearly so scrupulous in reproducing the repetitions of less conspicuous verbal details. His translation contains a few jarring examples of contemporary slang, such as "isn't that great," "Phooey!," "louse," and "goodies." Like Le Gallienne, he suppresses most of Nora's exclamations, either by omitting them or by rendering them in relatively tame English expressions—although he can also inconsistently intensify a rather moderate exclamation in the speeches of others. Worst of all, even though he usually succeeds in capturing the gist of a speech, like most of these translators he far too often fails to reproduce its characteristic phrasing. Krogstad's "You know, naturally, just as well as all the others, that I one time a few years ago happened to commit a thoughtless act," for example, appears in Reinert as "I'm sure you know, like everybody else, that some years ago I committed—an impropriety"; while Krogstad's "I can tell you that it was neither anything more nor anything worse which I once did and which destroyed my whole respectable standing" appears as "Let me tell you that what I did that time was no more and no worse. And it ruined my name and reputation."

These renderings exemplify the two primary sources of a pervasive looseness and approximation through which Reinert retains the gist of the original while constantly deviating from the original's articulation of that gist. The first source, minor but frequent, is the gratuitous dash creating a pause, usually of hesitation, where the original has none. The second, far more characteristic, is Reinert's tendency to devise two sentences for the original's one, often as a means of carrying over what in the original is a compound adjective. Here, chosen at random, are a few examples.

> KROGSTAD.   Even if you stood here with never mind how much cash in your hand, that wouldn't get you your note back from me.
> (Reinert: Even if you had the cash in your hand right this minute, I wouldn't give you your note back. It wouldn't make any difference *how* much money you offered me.) (act 2)

> NORA.   Yes, you see how necessary it is. You must instruct me right up to the end.
> (Reinert: Didn't I tell you I did? Now you've seen for yourself. I'll need your help till the very minute we're leaving for the party.) (act 2)

> HELMER.   That was really strikingly put. But don't you know what *you* ["du selv"—i.e., "you yourself"] want to be?
> (Reinert: Beautiful. Very good indeed. But how about yourself? Don't you know what you'll go as?) (act 3)

It is, especially, unnecessary looseness of this sort—which Reinert shares with Archer, Le Gallienne, and Meyer—that compels me to identify Rolf

Fjelde's version of *A Doll House* as unequivocally by far the best of the six. As noted, Fjelde's version has its limitations, but they are relatively minor and infrequent, especially when compared with the defects of the other five versions. Both Reinert's and Fjelde's versions are good for American readers and spectators because they avoid British expressions and achieve throughout a genuine American ring. But Fjelde's version is the best of the six, for Americans or for any English-speaking readers and spectators, because it is the most authentic. In comparing these six versions, I tried to note not only deviations from the original and problematic readings but also particularly successful renderings of passages difficult to convey in English—and most of the latter that I was able to note occur in Fjelde's version. To my mind, however, what especially gives Fjelde's version its authenticity and thus its great effectiveness is Fjelde's consistent and usually successful effort to retain not only the gist of the original but also its tone and rhythms. Whereas the other versions are far too loose, and often get looser as they go along, so that the characters tend to speak in the styles of their translators, the styles of speech we hear in Fjelde, though English rather than Norwegian, are usually those of the characters themselves. Fjelde's version is only a translation, not the original, and it's not even a perfect translation, but for the most part it provides about as good a rendering of *A Doll House* as we are likely to get. The English-speaking reader—or spectator—is fortunate to have it.

Required and Recommended Student Readings

The extent to which instructors recommend or assign readings varies greatly in the teaching of *A Doll House*. Naturally, there is a greater emphasis on background and complementary reading at upper-division and graduate levels. Nevertheless, there is a greater variation at the lower divisions than one might expect—the variations usually rising from the teacher's attitude rather than from differences in types of course. For example, some instructors in introductory English courses indicate that they prefer to present whatever background is needed, and some say that a formal introduction to the play closes off the analytical processes by providing the student with an interpretation. In contrast, other teachers in introductory English courses provide handouts and assign complementary plays for reading, as well as criticism, reviews of productions, and biographical material. The following discussion treats some of the materials that students are often encouraged or required to read. (A larger number of materials are discussed in the section "The Instructor's Library.")

It is obvious that Michael Meyer, *Ibsen: A Biography*, dominates the readings on Ibsen's life and career. The book is highly praised by critics and instructors and is often placed on reserve in the library. But the length and detail of this book lead to the inescapable conclusion that few students, at least at the undergraduate level, will read through it, and a number of shorter critical biographies are attractive alternatives. Two modern critical biographies used by instructors are Hans George Meyer, *Henrik Ibsen*, and Harold Clurman, *Ibsen*. Many instructors assign some combination of a shorter biography, the material specifically on *A Doll House* in Michael Meyer, and relevant excerpts from Evert Sprinchorn, ed., *Ibsen: Letters and Speeches*.

For background on the theater of Ibsen's time, Oscar G. Brockett, *History of the Theatre*, provides a good treatment of the theatrical events before and during the period in which Ibsen wrote his plays. Among more specialized studies, Stephen S. Stanton's useful and concise discussion of the well-made play in his introduction to Camille *and Other Plays* is very helpful for students who have little idea of the structure of a play and no vocabulary with which to discuss structure with any precision. Some instructors also assign one or more of the plays in Stanton's collection. Cary Mazer discusses the value of this assignment and gives a word of caution regarding the edition:

> I usually assign *A Glass of Water* by Scribe, a play which demonstrates all of the important features of the genre, and has the additional advantage of promoting a theme which justifies the laws of the dramatic form, namely that great historical events are caused by trivial incidents, much as the dramatic conflicts of the well-made play hinge upon in-

tercepted messages or, in this case, a spilled glass of water. Teachers and students alike should use the current edition with caution, being careful to restore the five-act structure, and to note the uncharacteristic additions to the *dénouement*. One must also prevent the students from getting the impression that well-made plays require an exotic, aristocratic historical setting (here, the court of Queen Anne), for they are just as often set in contemporary bourgeois Parisian households, where the material needs of the characters are in keeping with the genre's emphasis on physical objects and discrete packets of information.

Other plays by Ibsen are often assigned for reading along with *A Doll House*. *The Lady from the Sea* has many interesting parallels and the contrast of a reconciliation between the wife and husband. Many instructors assign the more familiar *Ghosts* and *Hedda Gabler*. Doris Lessing's short story "To Room Nineteen" is assigned by some instructors because of a similarity in subject matter.

Students who have little experience in analyzing plays as plays and who have seen few dramatic productions can learn a great deal by reading the chapter concerned with analyzing and directing *A Doll House* in Richard Hornby, *Script into Performance* (153–72). For information about present-day productions of *A Doll House* instructors assign reviews of the two recent movie versions.

Instructors often place several translations of *A Doll House* on reserve so that students may read introductory material written by such scholar-teachers as James Walter McFarlane, Rolf Fjelde, and Otto Reinert. Interpretative material is available in these introductions, as well as some stage history and commentary on the translation of the play.

That the question of feminism and *A Doll House* is clearly important today and of interest to students is indicated by comments from instructors in general survey courses as well as specialized courses in women's studies. Authors who treat this subject include Katharine Rogers, Elaine Hoffman Baruch, and others listed in the section "The Instructor's Library."

Although one instructor claims not to assign any critical material to students because "most of what was written about Ibsen was so weak," a close examination of the materials written about Ibsen, particularly in recent years, reveals that a wealth of sensitive, scholarly, and interesting material is available for the instructor who wishes to use it.

Aids to Teaching

Many factors influence instructors' use of teaching aids: the time available, the quality of the material, philosophical views about the value of audiovisual materials, and the instructor's facility with machinery. The subject is a volatile one, and survey responses reveal that while some instructors are merely indifferent to teaching aids, many are strongly pro or con.

Instructors favoring their use cite a wide range of methods and materials both inside and outside the classroom. Some show film versions of *A Doll House*; others show slides; still others use recordings of the play. Slides are preferred by most and are used in several ways for different types of classes. Richard Hornby (teaching in a school of theater) has assembled a set of slides that show the development of the box set and realistic scenery and their relation to the growth of realism in playwriting and in Ibsen's technique. Rolf Fjelde has compiled two formal slide presentations for use in various classes. He first presents "In Ibsen's World," which depicts Ibsen's social, historical, cultural, and theatrical milieu. Later in the course he shows "Ibsen in Performance," which shows interpretations of the play and different types of costumes and settings. One instructor emphasizes the deceptiveness of "realism" by showing slides of "realistic" paintings and discussing "non-realistic devices which give the painting structure and form. This helps students appreciate the extent to which Ibsen can be called 'realistic'—only with many qualifications." Imaginative slide showings of this kind can increase students' appreciation of the visual aspects of the play but take time for instructors to assemble and present. In less formal fashion, some instructors simply bring to class pictures and photographs of stage productions of *A Doll House*, of Norway, of Ibsen, and of the interiors of Norwegian houses (with such details as the tile stove, an important visual element in *A Doll House*).

Because of time limitations, few show films in class, but a number of instructors make films available, note their appearance on television or in a film series, or arrange showings outside of class. Two film versions of the play are mentioned with some frequency, although not always praised. Both alter the play considerably, and many feel that the balance of the play is lost because of too much focus on the Noras of Claire Bloom and Jane Fonda. Nevertheless, some instructors find that the films are useful in stimulating analysis and discussion. One respondent notes, "Though I disagree with both approaches, they generate lively discussions on the evenings when we view them." Another instructor reflects a general view of the Fonda film when he describes it as "particularly useful in discussing expository techniques, since the film dramatizes pre-play events." A third film is the Encyclopaedia Britannica's *A Doll's House*, narrated by Norris Houghton. A modern-dress film in two parts ("The Destruction of Illusion" and "Ibsen's Themes"), it runs a total of sixty-one minutes. Only two participants in the survey use it, one describing it as "dreadful, but with a few good scenes," while the other says he sometimes shows it to make a few points about "drab realism."

Some films other than those based on *A Doll House* have received a more favorable response. Some instructors who wish to expose students to additional plays by Ibsen have available videotapes of the BBC productions of *Hedda Gabler* and *The Wild Duck*, which are useful in showing Ibsen's theatrical techniques. A forty-one-minute color film used with enthusiasm by a few teachers is *Edvard Munch*, which provides background on Norway and on the artistic developments of the late nineteenth century. (Kenneth Clark described Munch as "the Ibsen of painting.")

Several instructors make available a Caedmon recording of *A Doll's House*, with Claire Bloom and Donald Madden. Lois More Overbeck places the recording on reserve in the library and asks students to listen to it, while following the text, for a second reading of the play. "The students enjoy the assignment, and they gain an interpretative reading of certain lines not apparent to them as silent readers."

Negative comments about the use of films and slides sometimes relate to the shortage of class time. *A Doll House* is often taught in survey courses, and instructors feel it is difficult to find enough time to provide material for background and for a thorough understanding of the play itself. Other courses allow time for such activities, but the teacher is philosophically opposed. In answer to the question, "What audiovisual materials do you find useful in teaching the play?" the following responses reflect the aversion of many instructors:

> NONE!!!! I don't as did one of my colleagues, flash a slide of a typical Norwegian house at the turn of the century. There is no limit to the foolishness of A-V.

> I rarely use A.V. materials; I try to get my kids to *think* and talk and write.

> I am not congenial to audiovisual machinery and feel freer without it. Besides, teaching the plays allows me the opportunity to do a dramatic reading, which I love.

> I'd rather have a student discover that his own mind is the greatest audio-visual aid.

In contrast to these differences of opinion, most teachers agree that the play should be explored *as a play*. Many use performance in the classroom and either organize or recommend student viewing of productions at the college or university or at local professional theaters. Some instructors find that performing sections of the play themselves is effective. Others find that having students read sections of the play aloud or perform scenes after rehearsing them and learning the lines increases understanding and ensures close analysis of the play. In one class, experienced actors performed scenes and discussed the play with the students. This is occasionally possible when there is a student production of an Ibsen play. Some instructors with the opportunity, time, and resources have videotaped rehearsal scenes as well as finished scenes of such productions to show their classes.

One respondent answered the question about aids to teaching, "Haven't used any. Any suggestions?" Many instructors would probably be interested in using aids that seem reasonable and not too time-consuming. Teaching aids can be a valuable part of a course, but they need to be handled carefully. Nothing is duller or more contrary to the spirit of a vital play of exploration like *A Doll House* than a series of deadly slides that bear little relation to the essence of the play. Handled well, however, slides, films, recordings, and performances can help students who have seen few plays and have little experience in visualizing a dramatic text. Many teachers remind us that *A Doll House* is very visual and that a fuller comprehension of the play emerges from an appreciation of the theatrical background and of the nuance and detail revealed through performance.

The Instructor's Library

A major element in recent Ibsen criticism is the growing awareness of the need for viewing any single play by Ibsen as part of a whole, an aspect of his total output, his life, his career, his philosophical views, as well as his relation to the theater he knew so well and so dramatically altered. Three factors have helped accelerate scholarship on *A Doll House*. One was the observance in 1978 of the sesquicentennial of Ibsen's birth, and it was followed in 1979 by the celebration of the centennial of the publication of *A Doll House*. The latter led to symposia, the publication of articles, and a large number of productions of the play. In addition, the number of new translations that have come out has not only demonstrated that the plays are by no means dated but also stimulated both new theatrical productions and new scholarship. Finally, the present concern with the position of women in society, the introduction of women's studies courses, and the development of the Women's Program in the American Theatre Association have focused attention on the play, which has come to symbolize the struggle for women's rights. The teacher approaching *A Doll House* will therefore find much scholarly material that is both challenging and controversial. The aim of this section is to direct the teacher to the areas available for research, not to provide synopses of the specific books, articles, and reviews.

This section focuses on published books, where much of the important Ibsen criticism has appeared. Beyond these books, however, is a broad area for study in the form of articles published in such journals as *Scandinavian Studies*, *Edda*, *Modern Drama*, *Theatre Journal*, *Essays in Theatre*, *PMLA*, *Literature in Performance*, and *Comparative Drama*. An annual publication founded in 1980 and devoted entirely to Ibsen is *Ibsen News and Comment: The Journal of the Ibsen Year in America* (Rolf Fjelde and Yvonne Shafer, eds., published by the Ibsen Society of America, Pratt Institute, Brooklyn, NY 11205). It contains interviews with Ibsen scholars, notable directors and designers, critics, and actors, as well as reviews of recent books on Ibsen and on past and current productions of his plays, reviews of current productions, and photographs of productions, scenery, and costume designs. Another yearly publication, *Ibsen Årbok*, edited by Einar Østvedt, contains essays by noted scholars. In the years in which there is an international Ibsen seminar in Oslo, the proceedings are published as both the *Ibsenåarboken* and *Contemporary Approaches to Ibsen*, edited by Daniel Haakonson, Einar Østvedt, and others.

Reference Works

A number of bibliographies will lead the instructor to many more books and articles than can be discussed in this volume. Ina Ten Eyck Firkins, *Ibsen:*

A Bibliography of Criticism and Bibliography, provides many entries on Ibsen in general and two pages of entries for early critical work on *A Doll House*. Annette Andersen, Sverre Arestad, and Milly S. Barranger guide the reader to more recent work, and annual bibliographies, compiled by Mariann Tiblin, Lise-Lone Marker, Harald S. Naess, and others appear in *Scandinavian Studies*. General bibliographies are also useful. Helen H. Palmer lists material in several languages including books, articles, and reviews of Ibsen's plays in *European Drama Criticism, 1900–1975*. The entries are organized under the title of the play, and there are thirty-six entries under *A Doll's House*. Irving Adelman and Rita Dworkin have ten pages of general entries on Ibsen in *Modern Drama: A Checklist of Critical Literature on Twentieth Century Plays*. There are eleven pages of entries on Ibsen and twenty-five entries under *A Doll's House. Dramatic Criticism Index*, edited by Paul F. Breed and Florence M. Sniderman, has several pages of general Ibsen entries and lists fifteen entries under *A Doll's House*. Some of the books cited below have very lengthy bibliographies, including work in several languages.

Background Studies

Many general books and specific studies provide information about the background of Ibsen's writing. Some of the areas that enhance understanding of the plays themselves are the development of modern drama, Ibsen's relation to Romanticism, changes in acting styles, the picture of Norwegian literature and theater of which Ibsen was a part, the philosophical movements that excited intellectuals in Scandinavia and Europe, and, closely related to the philosophical views, the changing political outlooks that provide a background for the action in many of Ibsen's plays.

Books about the development of modern drama and theater histories are recommended for a background on the theater preceding Ibsen's career, the theater of his time, and his impact on modern theater. Oscar Brockett, *History of the Theatre*, is a standard text used by many instructors. A picture of the British theater during the time Ibsen's plays were first produced in England appears in Bernard Shaw's *Our Theatres in the Nineties*. Other helpful books include John Gassner, *Masters of the Modern Drama*; Joseph Wood Krutch, *"Modernism" in Modern Drama: A Definition and an Estimate*; Storm Jameson, *Modern Drama in Europe*; Alvin Kernan, *Character and Conflict: An Introduction to Drama*; and Richard Gilman, *The Making of Modern Drama*.

Part of the development of modern drama was the reaction against Romanticism that dominated much of nineteenth-century theater. Some of Ibsen's plays are in the Romantic tradition, but he is most noted for the realistic plays that reject that mode of composition. Two excellent references on Romanticism are M. H. Abrams, *Natural Supernaturalism: Tradition and Revolution in Romantic Literature*, and Henry Aiken, *The Age of Ideology*.

The reaction against Romantic playwriting was paralleled by a reaction against Romantic acting techniques that were inappropriate for realistic plays. Works on approaches to acting that were being developed during Ibsen's career include Constantin Stanislavski, *An Actor Prepares, Building a Character*, and *Creating a Role*, and Richard Boleslavski, *Acting: The First Six Lessons*. Closely related to the development of realism in playwriting and acting was the emerging concept of costume design and the use of realistic clothing that visually conveyed the playwright's intentions. Lucy Barton, *Historic Costume for the Stage*, provides illustrations of the type of clothing worn by actors in performances of *A Doll House*.

Ibsen's relation with other Norwegian writers and his status in Norwegian artistic circles are described in a number of books. Brian W. Downs, *Modern Norwegian Literature*, provides background on Norwegian literature and on Ibsen's relation with Bjørnson and other Norwegian novelists and playwrights. In *The Genius of the Scandinavian Theatre* Evert Sprinchorn provides useful introductions to the plays of Ibsen and other Scandinavians as well as historically significant essays by several writers about Scandinavian literature. Essays about Ibsen and other Scandinavian writers are also found in James Walter McFarlane, *Ibsen and the Temper of Norwegian Literature*.

The philosophical aspects of Ibsen's plays are increasingly noted in criticism. Hans George Meyer, *Henrik Ibsen* places Ibsen in the tradition of Kant, Nietzsche, and Kierkegaard. Another important study, Brian Johnston's *The Ibsen Cycle*, contains an analysis of Hegel's philosophy as a background for Ibsen's plays. Søren Kierkegaard, *Either/Or*, is recommended by a number of instructors. A Kierkegaardian analysis of *A Doll House* as a basis for production of the play is presented in Richard Hornby, *Script into Performance*.

Both in contemporary productions and in contemporary criticism Ibsen's plays are often viewed as examples of a reaction against the complacent capitalist values of a bourgeois society. Useful economic and political material is found in Terry Eagleton, *Marxism and Literary Criticism*, and Fredric Jameson, *The Political Unconscious*. A study of the bourgeois life-style reflected in *A Doll House* is Peter Gay, *The Education of the Senses*, volume 1 of *The Bourgeois Experience*.

Biographies and Critical Studies

A complete study of *A Doll House* involves many significant areas of analysis and exploration. The major aspects of concern to the instructor, which are covered in the books and essays mentioned below, are biographical facts, the conventions of dramatic realism and the relation between Ibsen's drama and the popular theater of the nineteenth century, the theatrical impact of Ibsen's plays in production on audiences and critics, Ibsen's highly theatrical use of language, and the importance of *A Doll House* in relation to all of Ibsen's plays. A major area of critical interest is the impact of the social, historical, and philosophical questions that form the background of his plays and include the playwright's attitude toward feminism and the importance of *A Doll House* in the feminist movement. The books and essays that follow indicate the multifarious approaches that may be used in discussing *A Doll House*.

There are many sources for biographical material on Ibsen and on the actual people on whom he modeled Nora and other characters. The publication in 1971 of Michael Meyer's 865-page *Ibsen: A Biography* was a major event in Ibsen scholarship, and it is certainly essential reading for instructors of *A Doll House*. Moving from Ibsen's ancestry and childhood to the reactions to his death, Meyer presents a vivid and detailed account of Ibsen's development as a dramatist and of the circumstances regarding the writing, publication, and reception of each of the plays. A five-page selected bibliography lists materials Meyer drew on for this monumental study.

Meyer's work, however, should not turn instructors away from other helpful biographies, which differ in their emphases and points of view. For many years the standard biography of Ibsen was the distinguished Norwegian historian Halvdan Koht's *Life of Ibsen*, originally published in 1928–29 in commemoration of the centennial of Ibsen's birth. This book was revised and enlarged in 1954, in an edition then translated into English in 1971 by Einar Haugen and A. E. Santaniello. Other biographies recommended by instructors include Henrik Jaeger, *Henrik Ibsen 1828–1888*; Edmund Gosse, *Henrik Ibsen*; Francis Bull, *Ibsen: The Man and the Dramatist*; Harold Clurman, *Ibsen*; and Edvard Beyer, *Ibsen: The Man and His Work*. Information regarding Ibsen's life and artistic development is also provided in *Ibsen: Letters and Speeches*, edited by Evert Sprinchorn. A magnificently illustrated pictorial biography by Daniel Haakonsen, *Henrik Ibsen, mennesket og kunstneren*, is still available only in Norwegian but is an indispensable aid.

Ibsen's use of dramatic structure and his relation to other playwrights and standard playwriting techniques are important in understanding the dramatic means by which Ibsen conveyed his ideas to readers and audiences and at the same time revolutionized playwriting. Lists of works of criticism of this type deemed essential by Ibsen scholars and instructors frequently begin with John Northam, whose *Ibsen's Dramatic Method* and *Ibsen: A Critical Study* have contributed to broader and more challenging interpretations of Ibsen's playwriting. Many instructors teach *A Doll House* as an example of playwriting technique. One of the earliest books to focus on this important aspect was Peter Tennant's *Ibsen's Dramatic Technique*. Other relevant discussions include Stephen S. Stanton's introduction to Camille *and Other Plays*; Brander Matthews, *Papers on Playmaking*; Donald Clive Stuart, *The Development of Dramatic Art*; and "The Well-Made Play" by Simon Williams. For an analysis of Ibsen's use of retrospective structure, the instructor may consult the chapter on *Rosmersholm* in Thomas Van Laan, *The Idiom of Drama*. For studying the structure of *A Doll House*, the notes and drafts Ibsen made are very helpful, and these may be found in James Walter McFarlane, *The Oxford Ibsen*, and William Archer, ed., *From Ibsen's Workshop: Notes, Scenarios, and Drafts of the Modern Plays*.

An important factor in Ibsen's dramatic technique is his highly effective, theatrical use of language. The instructor reading about *A Doll House* will encounter many discussions of language and of the subtle richness and humor of Ibsen's plays in Norwegian. One recommended article is Inga-Stina Ewbank, "Ibsen's Dramatic Language as a Link between His 'Realism' and His 'Symbolism.' " For instructors who wish to examine the linguistic patterns in *A Doll House* in the original Norwegian or compare translations and passages, two books are of assistance: Einar Haugen and Kenneth G. Chapman, *Spoken Norwegian*, and Haugen, *Norwegian-English Dictionary*.

Of course the language and the dramatic technique used by Ibsen can only be fully appreciated in production. Much recent scholarship has emphasized the theatrical aspects of Ibsen's plays. Increasing attention has been given to the plays as pieces of theater, and many now feel that in the past too much emphasis was placed on thematic elements of the play. Today more instructors focus on the dramaturgical elements of the play that convey Ibsen's outlook on society. The papers from the 1978 Ibsen conference at the University of British Columbia in Vancouver have been published in *Ibsen and the Theatre: The Dramatist in Production*, edited by Errol Durbach. A book emphasizing performance aspects of the plays is Richard Hornby, *Script into Performance: A Structuralist View of Play Production*, which contains a chapter on *A Doll House*. Einar Haugen, *Ibsen's Drama: Author to Audience*, is a study of the plays as communication, based on Roman Jakobson's six-sided model. The problems of American producers in Ibsen's time are amusingly indicated in Haugen's "Ibsen in America," an account of the first American (Milwaukee) production in 1882. Danish performances of Ibsen's plays from 1973 to 1978, including two productions of *A Doll House*, are reviewed in Ulla Strømberg and Jytte Wiingaard, eds., *Den levende Ibsen*. A very useful overview of the criticism of Ibsen's plays as they appeared, with reprints of reviews and articles, is *Ibsen: The Critical Heritage*, edited by Michael Egan.

Whether the focus is on production history, thematic elements, or dramatic technique, Ibsen's plays are most clearly understood in relation to the whole body of his writing. This point is emphasized in many of the books above and in Brian Johnston, *The Ibsen Cycle* and *To the Third Empire*. An understanding of the relation among the plays is also enhanced by a number of collections that bring together important recent criticism, along with notable essays from the past. Two of the collections most often recommended are *Discussions of Henrik Ibsen*, edited by James Walter McFarlane, and *Ibsen: A Collection of Critical Essays*, edited by Rolf Fjelde.

Naturally many works of criticism cover several aspects of Ibsen's work, combining an analysis of his technique with significant biographical factors and, at the same time, placing major emphasis on the relation between Ibsen's plays and historical, intellectual, and philosophical influences. The books cover a wide scope in time as well as in approach to *A Doll House*, demonstrating once again the multiple possibilities for analysis. Most often recommended for study are Muriel C. Bradbrook, *Ibsen, the Norwegian: A Revaluation*; Eric Bentley, *The Playwright as Thinker* and *In Search of Theatre*; and G. Wilson Knight, *Henrik Ibsen*. These books made a profound impression when they were written, called attention to the breadth of Ibsen's work, and have continued to maintain an important place in Ibsen scholarship. Other similarly important works are Maurice Valency, *The Flower and the Castle*; Robert Brustein, *The Theatre of Revolt*; F. L. Lucas, *The Drama of Ibsen and Strindberg*; Francis Fergusson, *The Idea of a Theatre*; Charles R. Lyons, *Henrik Ibsen: The Divided Consciousness*; Richard Hornby, *Patterns in Ibsen's Middle Plays*; and Theodore Jorgenson, *Henrik Ibsen: A Study in Art and Personality*. Books relating particular Ibsen plays to particular aspects of society (such as the significance of capitalism) include Bernard F. Dukore, *Money and Politics in Ibsen, Shaw, and Brecht*; Orley I. Holtan, *Mythic Patterns in Ibsen's Last Plays*; James Hurt, *Catiline's Dream*; Brian W. Downs, *A Study of Six Plays by Ibsen*; and Adolf E. Zucker, *Ibsen: The Master Builder*.

Probably the most famous of Ibsen critics has been George Bernard Shaw, but there is a division of opinion about Shaw's evaluation of the plays: some feel he reinforces the tendency to consider them with too narrow a focus on the social comment, whereas others find his criticism essential to the study of Ibsen. The new edition of Shavian commentary edited by J. L. Wisenthal, *Shaw and Ibsen: Bernard Shaw's* The Quintessence of Ibsenism, provides insights into the social and philosophical struggles that were taking place when the plays were written.

Another social issue related to Ibsen's plays is feminism. There are strongly opposed opinions about the amount of feminism in *A Doll House* and about Ibsen's attitude toward Nora. These subjects are discussed in articles and books by Elizabeth Hardwick, Elaine Hoffman Baruch, Elenore Lester,

Katharine M. Rogers, Marvin Rosenberg, Richard F. Dietrich, Otto Heller, and, in one of the most controversial books on Ibsen, Hermann J. Weigand.

Space limitations preclude the inclusion of all the valuable essays on Ibsen in recent years, or even of those dealing directly with *A Doll House*. Survey participants singled out those by Robert Brustein ("Crack"), Arthur Ganz, James Kerans, Eva Le Gallienne ("Ibsen, the Shy Giant"), Frederick Marker and Lise-Lone Marker, John Northam ("Ibsen's Search"), and, in an essay highly praised by many instructors, Evert Sprinchorn ("Ibsen and the Actors").

Part Two

APPROACHES

INTRODUCTION

There is no single way to teach *A Doll House*. Many factors affect the analysis and presentation of this richly constructed play. The essays in this volume discuss various levels of interpretation and a range of teaching approaches. As Barry Witham puts it, the play may be viewed through many different lenses, including feminism, structuralism, and Marxism. In selecting essays for the book, I looked for diversity not only in types of classes but especially in interpretation and approach. Each teacher views the play from a particular perspective, influenced by cultural, political, social, and philosophical interests, so that (as one reader suggested) the text "becomes a different artifact in the hands of a teacher, just as it becomes a different object in the theater with each interpretation." Space limitations permitted only a sampling of the many valid approaches available.

The instructors who have written the essays teach in many different types of departments, including departments of English, theater, comparative literature, humanities, and a school of theater and a performance-interpretation center. They teach at undergraduate and graduate levels, for majors and nonmajors. Specific courses include Freshman Introduction to Composition and Literature, College Composition (freshman honors course), Introduction to Literature (freshmen), Modern Drama (sophomores), Play Analysis (undergraduate English majors), Modern European Drama (seniors), Modern Drama (juniors and seniors), Dramatic Literature (undergraduate English majors and nonmajors), Analysis and Performance—Modern Drama: Chekhov, Ibsen, Shaw (undergraduate theater majors), Ibsen/Strindberg (juniors and seniors), and Seminar in Ibsen (graduates). *A Doll House* is taught in connection with other plays of Ibsen, with the work of other playwrights, and with novels, short stories, and poems.

In the first essay, Lois More Overbeck describes her use of the play in an introductory course as a means of helping students understand close analytical reading and recognize that "even criticism must be read critically." Sverre Lyngstad discusses his treatment of the play in a course in which the students explore the various genres of literature and develop explication and analysis skills. Approaching her introductory course through a discussion of genres, Joanne Gray Kashdan emphasizes the psychological aspects of the play and focuses on the interpretation of character. At a more advanced level, Otto Reinert outlines three lectures densely packed with material about the play and its background. June Schlueter also teaches an upper-division course and introduces some welcome humor into the study of the play as "a model for the creation of character and dramatic action." Again at the upper-division level, Cary Mazer relates Ibsen's playwriting technique to the well-made play, and Barry Witham and John Lutterbie use the play to teach a Marxist analysis of literature. In a course that explores women's traditional familial roles, Katharine Rogers relates the play to other novels and plays in which women are significant. Irving Deer examines the play as a process of growth and self-understanding for both Nora and Torvald. J. L. Styan describes how he uses performance of the play to enhance understanding, detailing a method that would be appropriate for many different types of courses, and Gay Gibson Cima and David Downs respectively describe the value of a performance approach in an English course and in an acting program. Brian Johnston relates the play to Ibsen's work as a whole, emphasizing philosophical aspects and an analysis of Ibsen's language. Richard Hornby discusses the large body of background material needed for a graduate course and specific questions used to spark a meaningful discussion of the play.

A major theme in the essays is the need for a broad view of the play and a condemnation of a static approach. Complexity, ambiguity, and transition are important both in interpretation and in teaching approaches. The play itself is seen, as Hornby puts it, as a play of transformation. Likewise, it has been viewed in many ways in different historical periods, as Lyngstad describes in his overview of the critical response. The essays also focus on the need to consider A Doll House as a play and to emphasize the dramatic effects and semiotic elements, remembering, as J. L. Styan remarks, that Ibsen engages us "in the proper business of the theater."

Despite these common views, there are considerable differences in the interpretations of the play. Recent criticism of Ibsen's work has moved away from the standard view of A Doll House as a one-thesis play constructed in black and white terms and as possibly passé because of changes in society. In place of this simplistic view, the essays forcefully indicate the many facets that the play reveals on close examination. Johnston explores a dialectical vision of reality, emphasizing the archetypal and ritualist dimension of the play, whereas Rogers explores contemporary social implications, and Witham looks at the symbolism of the bank and the significance of the role of money.

A feminist approach to the play has aroused fresh controversy. This aspect is stressed by Rogers, but other instructors object to recent reductionist views of the play as a feminist drama. Hornby begins his class discussion with the question, How much feminism is there in A Doll House? Deer focuses on the uncertainty of Nora's position and the ambiguity in the play, and Reinert entitles a section of his lectures "Beyond Feminism." Most of the essays suggest that a discussion of the play's connection with feminism has value if it is properly channeled and kept firmly linked to Ibsen's text.

Differences in structure, objectives, and the level of students mean that courses are organized differently. Several of the instructors, like Mazer, Deer, and Overbeck, use the play as a model for understanding the process of close analysis and then studying works by Strindberg, Wedekind, Maeterlinck, Chekhov, and others. Schlueter teaches the play early in the course, calling it "the best initiation into drama I know." Hornby moves into a discussion of *A Doll House* after several weeks of reading and talking about Ibsen's life and career, historical background, and philosophical and artistic movements. Although survey courses have to cover a great deal of material, some instructors organize the course so that a large amount of time is spent on *A Doll House*. In her introductory course in a two-year community college, Kashdan devotes one three-hour evening session to the play. In another introductory course, in a women's liberal arts college, Overbeck spends two weeks on the play, using it to teach students to analyze texts closely. Downs, who teaches a three-year program in actor training, uses the play in a gradual process that moves from improvised scenes through a formal presentation of scenes. Schlueter and Hornby allow from three to six fifty-minute classes, depending on how stimulating and valuable the discussion is.

Pedagogical methods range from Reinert's lectures aimed at the student who "has some idea of what drama is" and Johnston's lecture-discussion classes with students who have usually taken his graduate course in Romantic drama, to the rehearsal and performance of scenes from the play used by Cima and Downs. Discussion is especially appropriate for a playwright who used discussion in an innovative and startling manner. Hornby suggests several ways to improve the level of class discussion, noting the importance of a strong framework and a fresh and vital view of the play. Kashdan has found that listening to tapes made by students during the discussion helps her improve the level of discussion. Many of the instructors place materials on reserve for the students; Kashdan provides a six-page handout on psychological approaches and recommends two relevant films shown on cable television and available at little expense on VCR. Overbeck and Cima show the filmed versions of the play, emphasizing the differences between the play and the films, and Overbeck makes a recording of the play available to her students. Kashdan reads a play, Claire Booth Luce's "A Doll House 1970," as an introduction to the study of Ibsen's play (a useful means of providing variety in a three-hour class). Other instructors, including Styan, find it valuable to perform scenes from the play themselves or to have student actors perform scenes. In Downs's course background material for the play is turned into improvised scenes in class.

Instructors give various types of writing assignments to help students learn to analyze plays and to understand literature. Mazer, emphasizing the structure of the play, asks students to diagram the play and to write new scenarios for Ibsen's plays or other well-made plays, in order to understand *numérotage*; and Downs asks each student to keep a journal noting responses to the play and to background material. Hornby encourages the students to mark their copies of the play liberally with notes and comments and has them list the use of properties, costumes, sound effects, and setting in *A Doll House*. Assignments outside of class include trips to museums in Downs's course and to film showings in Cima's course.

Most of the instructors evaluate the students on the basis of papers, and some on the basis of class discussion and in-class writing assignments as well. The papers take various forms. Lyngstad often encourages students in his honors course to compare characters from *A Doll House* with those in *Hedda Gabler*. Cima's students write essays interpreting the scene that is performed and justifying the interpretation on the basis of an analysis of the play, reviews, books, and articles. Kashdan gives an essay examination at the end of the unit on *A Doll House*.

The fourteen instructors represented in this volume find Ibsen's play vital, exciting, and beautifully constructed. A significant element in the development of modern drama, *A Doll House* is also relevant to economic and social realities today. The high literary quality and complex design of the play are attested by its use in many different courses by instructors in many different fields.

INTRODUCTORY COURSES IN LITERATURE AND COMPOSITION

From Relevance to Critical Thinking: The Critical Difference

Lois More Overbeck

Most of my undergraduates have thoroughly enjoyed reading *A Doll House*. Some of this pleasure comes from the timeliness of its issues, but as we read the play even greater interest arises from the timelessness of the play. To be sure, the play reflects feminism's concern with liberating women from restrictive marital and social roles. And, more broadly, Nora's circumstances might remind students of their own need to evaluate the expectations imposed by others. But *A Doll House* is not only a play about Nora the oppressed woman or Nora the rebel breaking away from the past and finding the freedom to be herself. It is a play about the human endeavor to determine value and commitment.

Nora is disabused of her illusions when they are undermined by experience, just as Torvald understands the miracle only after she has abandoned him. But neither the specific illusions of Nora nor the ideals that blind Torvald constitute the whole point of *A Doll House*; instead, through dramatic irony we recognize the inadequacy of codifying our response to experience or our place in any human relationship.

35

The starting point for discovery of these broader perspectives is in the play's relevance. Just as metaphor compares the unfamiliar to the known, so relevance provides the familiar element that helps students discover greater depths of knowing. When we speak of relevance in this way, we are actually suggesting that literature endures because it embodies truths of the human condition. Through a play like *A Doll House*, students learn to understand this function of literature while they also grow in self-understanding. Hence *A Doll House* is an effective part of a freshman introductory course in literature and composition.

Because I teach the play early in an introductory course that is organized generically and because students' identification with issues of the play often keeps them from considering the dramatic tensions in the character of Nora and in the plot itself, I stress the dramaturgy of *A Doll House* to make students aware of a three-dimensional experience emanating from the text. A primary goal of our introductory course is close analytical reading of literary texts, so I have developed a sequence of assignments that encourage them to reread the play for specific writing tasks. These written preparations for class discussion guide students to a more refined understanding of the text and ask them to consider their own responses to the play in a continually recursive process of discovery.

Students are expected to have read the play before our first meeting. I begin the class by asking them to define briefly, in writing, the dramatic question of *A Doll House*. Some of their responses concern plot. Will Torvald find out? Will he reject or support Nora when he does? Others focus on character. Will Nora come back? If so, as a wife or as a new woman? Can Torvald achieve the miracle, can he change? Although identification with Nora seems inevitable, many students still want Nora's expectation of a miracle to be fulfilled, for they may not be willing themselves to take the irrevocable step that Nora has taken. Almost all students seem comfortable responding to the play with a statement of dramatic question, indicating that they will be open to exploring meaning as they study the play.

To prepare for the first discussion, I ask for a brief written study of the exposition of a character in act 1. (Characters are individually assigned so that several students are prepared on each; in larger classes, I would ask students to compare notes in small groups before I began class discussion.) By focusing on the dramaturgy of exposition, students distinguish *what* they know about a character from *how* they know it. A lively class discussion ensues as observations accumulate: Nora overtips; she stealthily checks Torvald's whereabouts before indulging in a macaroon, and yet she casually lies about it; she tosses her head when she tries to repress an unwonted reality; she is constantly moving; she uses multiple voices with Torvald; when acquiescent, she often has her back to Torvald or averts her eyes. Frequently observations about one character reveal something about another, so interruptions intensify the dynamics of discussion. Out of the abundance of detail, I can readily demonstrate the significance of gesture, stage movement, setting as imagery, and subtle shifts of characterization that occur with each change in the composition of the group of characters on stage. And from such concrete observations, I can compare Ibsen's dramaturgy with that of the well-made play; without elaborately discussing the history of the theater, it is possible to illustrate Ibsen's contribution to modern drama.

For the next class, students consider how a single character differs in act 1 and act 3 (each student writes on a new character, individually assigned). Students review the text to find detailed examples and then generalize about the changes and continuities of characterization. The results of this assignment often surprise them: for students whose initial reading had suggested a sudden change in Nora's character in act 3, the reconsideration demonstrates that Nora's discontent festers beneath the surface from the beginning. Students see that Nora is complex and that the tension of the play resides in her character as much as it does in the external circumstances of plot. Torvald too is seen as more than merely the villain of an oppressed household or a symbol of a repressed society. As one student observed in her paper, Torvald is acting out of defensiveness and weakness, characteristics that are evident quite early in the play; although he claims principles about money and gains Nora's submission to his will, he gives her the money she seeks; he also exposes the fragility of his newly acquired middle-class authority, for he feels threatened by Krogstad's familiarity. These details, together with numerous examples of Torvald's delicacy of taste, suggest a man whose actions are governed by appearances. In short, his obsessions are less a matter of principle than a defensive insecurity. So when Torvald (act 3) offers Nora social respectability despite her unforgivable lapse, he is acting despotically and yet perfectly in character. The shock with which Nora and the audience recoil is a necessary impetus for the change that enables Nora to conceive of an alternative to such a relationship.

By considering character as action, our class discussion of plot quickly moves beyond mechanical questions, such as whether Torvald will discover the secret, to questions of why Nora would let Torvald discover the letter and force a confrontation. Students realize that Ibsen's characters are not merely exemplars of social mores but complex figures whose actions bear on the actions of others. This perception enables students to discuss their dramatic expectations and the effect of dramatic reversals on their responses to the play.

The third class focuses on character foils (Torvald and Dr. Rank, Torvald and Krogstad, Mrs. Linde and Nora, Nora and Krogstad, Nora and Dr. Rank, Torvald-Nora and Krogstad–Mrs. Linde). Although each student treats one pair for an assignment intended as brief preparation for class discussion, most students elaborate beyond that limited topic because the comparisons of characters lead them to see a patterning of action as well. From specific observation, the class moves comfortably to generalization, and then to an aesthetic appreciation of Ibsen's dramaturgy. One student wrote of the dramaturgy of contrast: "It is really through Mrs. Linde that we can see how unrealistic and sheltered Nora is. . . . Both women are powerful: Mrs. Linde . . . by being assertive, Nora . . . by being submissive." Yet the student also saw inversion as the pattern of the play: "Independent Mrs. Linde wants to marry Krogstad and have something to live for. Dependent Nora wants to leave her family in order to have some meaning in her life" (Beth Hutchinson, untitled, unpublished paper, 1983). Similarly, Torvald and Krogstad seem to be good versus evil, to listen to Torvald's assessment and Dr. Rank's echo of it; however, students easily perceive the inversion of the play's action, for Krogstad makes amends for his behavior and finds happiness in Mrs. Linde's unconditional love, whereas Torvald is left confused and alone. This assignment shows students that their first impressions undergo change as they experience the play.

Along with such patterns of inverted expectation, students find parallelism. Nora is the shadow of Krogstad; each time Torvald denounces the sins of the reprobate, we see the dramatic irony with which Nora recognizes her own course. Nora is also like Dr. Rank in her sense of an impending doom from which there is no escape; this feeling is reinforced by the imagery of illness and moral decay. Rank's last celebration of life is followed by a final separation foreshadowing Nora's departure. Just as Nora's sensitivity is heightened by her own dreaded circumstances following the gaiety of the tarantella, so is Torvald's diminished by his impatience. Thus Dr. Rank's departure scene consists of cross talk that the audience perceives as dramatic irony; its function is to allow our simultaneous perception of three perspectives. Later, when Nora expects the miracle that Torvald does not understand, the irony of cross talk repeats, deepened in significance because of its dramaturgical and thematic parallelism to the earlier scene. Throughout, dramatic irony causes the audience to feel the discrepancy between what Nora feels and what Torvald perceives. We can anticipate the failure of the miracle, although, like Nora, we would prefer illusion to such confrontation with reality. When students consider the dramatic function of foils, they see that Ibsen has created a complex web of expectation that, together with dramatic irony, transfers to the audience the dramatic tension within the play.

Within a week's study, students have reread parts of the play three times to prepare brief and cumulative written assignments. From such close reading, they have made detailed observations, extrapolated generalizations, and gained awareness of the dramatic texture of the play that will help them to be more critical when they consider the intellectual and cultural backgrounds of *A Doll House* and the responses to it. Now they select a topic for an analytical paper. To help them reexperience the play as a whole, I suggest that they listen to the recording of the Claire Bloom performance; reviewing the play helps them to consolidate their impressions and make a commitment to their own responses before becoming involved in critical interpretations. I suggest that, as they listen to the play, they note examples that will support their ideas. Writing out their thoughts in this way seems to help students be more critical and selective in their use of secondary sources.

The paper on *A Doll House* incorporates some controlled reading of critical responses to the play. Part of this assignment is designed to prepare students for the writing of a critical term paper, but I find that the results justify the assignment as a useful approach to *A Doll House*. I deliberately assign six essays that present conflicting interpretations of the play (many other essays might serve a similar purpose). Students read and briefly summarize the controlling idea and bases of support for each essay; these summaries help them separate their ideas from those of the critics. Because they have had time to develop their ideas inductively from close reading of the play, students are prepared to read critics critically: they either challenge the arguments they read or are challenged by them to examine their own ideas more comprehensively. In their papers, students must formulate their own interpretation of a single character in comparison to several critical interpretations; such a requirement helps them find an argumentative edge for their paper, which they are better able to reason closely.

Hermann J. Weigand, *The Modern Ibsen: A Reconsideration*, labels Nora comic, claiming that she lacks the courage for suicide and that her faith in the miracle is a response of hysteria. Although he recognizes the sham of Torvald's heroism, Weigand's sympathy rests with Torvald, who knew nothing of the circumstances of the forgery. Weigand asserts that Nora still playacts at the end and will probably return home when she tires of this new game. Elaine Hoffman Baruch, "Ibsen's *Doll House*: A Myth for Our Time," believes the play embodies feminism and a new myth for women. She suggests that both Nora and Torvald see their illusions broken, but that Nora is tragic for she (like Antigone) is beset by conflicting claims of family, self, and law. Baruch warns that the modern audience cannot assume that it is free of such illusions. Elenore Lester, "Ibsen's Unliberated Heroines," surveys Ibsen's female characters who "live through men" and finds that only Nora chooses to be independent (58–59). She offers a social history of Ibsen's creation of the figure of Nora that demonstrates that *A Doll House* appeared at the right moment to mark "the beginning of an era in woman's history" (60). From an apparently chauvinist view to feminist ones, these three essays offer a range of interpretations that respond to the temper of their times as well as to the play.

Following such dialectic, students appreciate H. L. Mencken's straightforward introduction to *Eleven Plays of Henrik Ibsen*. Mencken responds to the scandal of the original production by affirming that Ibsen was a respectable man whose chief interest was "not with the propagation of ethical ideas, but with the solution of aesthetic problems" (x–xi). Ibsen poses questions about human emotions and destinies present in social conditions and principles instead of attempting to answer them (xiv). Mencken also demonstrates Ibsen's dramaturgical innovations by comparing Ibsen's realistic situations, characters, and actions with those of the well-made play. Marvin Rosenberg, "Ibsen vs. Ibsen or: Two Versions of *A Doll's House*," contrasts two drafts of the play that show the duality of Ibsen as artist and social thinker. The first draft, the thinker's play, has long set pieces on social issues; Torvald is at first solicitous, then condemning, and Nora leaves. In the second draft, nuances of appearance and reality are developed, Dr. Rank's illness shadows the whole play with death, Torvald is cowardly and arrogant, Nora matures to give up her concealment: plot gives way to character. The second draft veers from women's rights to become a play about failed individuals; Nora still leaves, but her recognition that Torvald is corrupt suggests to Rosenberg that, in character, Nora might not have left her children to Torvald's influence. Finally, Evert Sprinchorn, "Ibsen and the Actors," considers theatrical interpretations to illumine characterization of Nora as a divided soul. In many modern performances characters have been reduced to caricature: thus Nora becomes a star vehicle and Torvald a villain (although Torvald was played originally by Gustaf Fredrikson, a leading actor of Ibsen's day). Sprinchorn asserts that Nora's role is distorted by such interpretations and her complexity as a character is sacrificed. He confirms Ibsen's intent to make "good drama with living persons" rather than create characters who embody ideas. The range of these three essays is helpful in establishing the need to separate Ibsen the writer from Ibsen as representative of his era; this, in turn, demonstrates the need to consider the play as more than a statement for cherished opinions of our own time.

None of these essays wholly satisfies the students, who can see the reasonableness of inherently conflicting positions. Class discussion provides a forum for some of the difficult and perhaps unanswerable questions. Did Nora make a choice or was she driven by circumstance? Could she have changed herself or Torvald when she realized the impossibility of holding a romantic ideal as her standard; could she, as Mrs. Linde did Krogstad, accept Torvald or change him? Sprinchorn and Baruch both mention draft versions and alternative endings of *A Doll House*; these shifts of textual emphasis are provocative, but such speculative discussions must be grounded in a close reading of the text. Never is this more vivid than in the students' reaction to the film version, *A Doll's House*, directed by Joseph Losey (with Jane Fonda, David Warner, and Trevor Howard); students were frustrated by the film's infidelity to the text, particularly when rearranged sequences invalidated character and motive and when extraliterary scenic effects subtracted the evocative metaphor of the confined stage setting.

One reason that I take two weeks for this approach to *A Doll House* is to challenge students to hold their own readings of a text on a plane with those of critics. When conflicting interpretations make them realize that even criticism must be read critically, they are in a position to learn from their reading as well as to form and modify their own judgments. Is *A Doll House* a text worthy of this time and emphasis? I think it is uniquely so because the play is thematically relevant to the intellectual experience that students have in studying it. Both Nora and Torvald hold unexamined beliefs that govern their lives even when conflicting experiences impinge on and eventually undermine their illusions. The dramaturgy of the play (dramatic irony, masquerading, doubling) helps the audience see these discrepancies even before the characters recognize a need to abandon illusion and take a wider view of their reality. Hence the audience experiences both empathy and distance in response to the work.

Moreover, students see the emotional validity of the play both in their own terms and in terms of historical perspective. They need the distance that the critical assignment helps them discover. They also need to realize that their own responses are complex: as one student commented, "I can feel the fear, disappointment and courage Nora is experiencing" (Kimberly Williams, untitled, unpublished essay). Studying *A Doll House* does make a critical difference. It helps students to understand the commonality of human experience expressed in literature and also to recognize the biases that they bring from their own lives to any new experience.

Ibsen in the Freshman Honors Course

Sverre Lyngstad

Ibsen's plays can be used to advantage in several types of college composition courses. *A Doll's House*, for example, lends itself superbly to a course organized around women's studies, as has been shown by the German critic Heistrüvers. It has been equally successful as the first play studied in my course Composition and Literature at New Jersey Institute of Technology, which introduces students to literature through a selection of modern stories, plays, and poems, in that order. I have tried to choose drama texts representing various modes and styles, while maintaining a balance between European and American selections. Most recently, I have combined two Ibsen plays, *A Doll's House* and *Hedda Gabler*, with Miller's *A View from the Bridge* and Williams's *A Streetcar Named Desire*.

The goal of the literary component of the course is twofold: (1) to provide the students with the experience of literature in its various genres and (2) to help them develop skills of literary explication and analysis.

I start with a brief discussion of the languages of science, journalism, and poetry—abstract and precise; objective and factual; subjective, often ambiguous and allusive, respectively. While students are aware that literature has an emotive quality, they need to be reminded that the world recreated by the artist also often has a visionary aspect, which requires from the reader a freshness of seeing not easy to maintain amid a daily bombardment of stereotypes and clichés. Moreover, in order to share their responses with others, the students must learn to conceptualize their literary perceptions. To facilitate this process, a critical text is assigned, Sylvan Barnet's *A Short Guide to Writing about Literature*, which also provides an elementary "theory of literature" appropriate to college freshmen.

A brief discussion of mimesis helps to focus students' attention on another aspect of the literary work, its relation to so-called reality. Some authors seem to reproduce the flux of experience; others shape stylized patterns and artificial forms. The degree and kind of manipulation of experience result in distinct literary styles: classicism, realism, impressionism, expressionism, and so forth. To illustrate the implications of style, how it affects every single aspect of a literary work (plot, character portrayal, image motifs, treatment of time, etc.), two stories are initially assigned for comparison and contrast, Maupassant's "The Jewels" and Chekhov's "Gooseberries." Similar contrasts are also noted for the drama.

In my syllabus, *A Doll's House* is given three to four fifty-minute periods, divided into class discussion, lecture, and an occasional scene reading. By way of introduction, I remind the students of the chief characteristics of drama as a genre and explain the theory behind the theater of realism.

Students will be familiar with the idea of impersonation, or enactment: drama is usually written to be performed and seen. They may be less aware of the constraints this intention imposes on the playwright, who is limited to a single presentational form—dialogue—and to a work length determined by the attention span—roughly two hours—of the theater-going public. I find it helpful to stress the enforced economy that this temporal restriction entails: no word can be wasted, every entrance and exit must be weighed. By compensation, the playwright can develop the element of spectacle, by utilizing scenic design, lighting, dance, and other arts. Ibsen exploits several of these devices in A Doll's House, thereby making his play visually exciting.

As a background to the theater of realism, I define the various concepts of the stage, bringing out in particular the implicit relationship between the audience and the stage. Students are invited to share my puzzled amusement over the so-called fourth-wall convention, a weird paradox of the realistic theater, turning the audience into inadvertent spies on intimate scenes of everyday life. (They will appreciate the attempts of other dramatists studied, such as Tennessee Williams, to eliminate this artificial wall between stage and audience in the realistic theater.) This convention is then related to the intent of that theater, namely, to produce an illusion of reality. Curiously, though, Ibsen's realistic drama is anything but lifelike—it is highly condensed, meticulously crafted, and charged with ideas. Nonetheless, it does evoke an illusion of reality—as does Hemingway's fiction with its artificial, stylized dialogue.

Ibsen's carefully wrought, compact dramatic form stems partly from the model of the well-made play, partly from the analytic structure that he developed. The scrupulously prepared entrances, emphatic curtains, surprise endings, and suspense—all these elements derive from the mechanics of the well-made play. Still, as Donald Clive Stuart has noted, A Doll's House is "more than a perfect machine. It is a living organism" (580). Students will perceive how this stereotype of nineteenth-century entertainment, with its hackneyed device of revelation of long-hidden secrets, in Ibsen's hands becomes charged with dramatic vitality. Because Ibsen "saw life itself as a placid surface through which, from time to time, what seemed dead and buried will break—a present into which the 'vanished' past returns"— with him this pattern, as well as the retrospective structure he brought to such perfection, turned into the "instrument of a vision" (Bentley, Search 351–52). The outcome of the unveiling of such secrets, along with ever deeper layers of the past, is reminiscent of Sophoclean tragedy.

In preparation for teaching A Doll's House as tragedy, I briefly comment on typical, historically determined kinds of tragic predicament in literature, while stressing the relatively unchanging nature of the tragic experience. The class will be familiar with the concept of fate as an expression of indomitable forces that no mortal can fight with impunity. They will note how

Ibsen secularized these forces, which in his plays appear as circumstance, heredity, the social structure. Yet he, too, creates the sense of inevitability, or necessity, which the tragic form demands. In *A Doll's House* the antagonistic force irrupts from the outside world, from society; its vehicle is Krogstad's intrigue, with its whiff of melodrama. But the melodramatic devices used—repeated knocks at the door and rings of the doorbell, and the to-do about the mailbox—are absorbed by the sphere of intense feeling that surrounds Nora's embattled secret. The play's tragic quality arises largely from the passionate commitment with which Nora, like Antigone, fights the relentless forces that threaten to destroy her world and from the disproportionately high cost, in terms of renunciation and suffering, of her exit to freedom.

Since we go through the play act by act and scene by scene, I provide a frame for the chronological examination by presenting in advance an overarching concept of the dramatic action. To this end, I use Francis Fergusson's idea of the tragic rhythm, with its three phases: purpose, passion, and perception (*Idea* 18). Accordingly, the class discussion focuses on Nora. It is she whose plans for a carefree future (purpose) are in act 1 constantly being interrupted by the ringing of the bell, causing abysses, of both the past and the future, to open up before her. The transition to the phase of passion, or suffering, occurs at the end of act 1, where Nora begins to fear that she may "poison" her home and her children. The phase of passion extends throughout act 2 and part of act 3, at which point Nora's new perception shatters her existence.

In the discussion of Nora, called by Evert Sprinchorn the "richest, most complex" female dramatic character since the heroines of Shakespeare ("Ibsen and the Actors" 125), a key question concerns the motivation of her radical change in act 3. To sharpen students' focus, the instructor may give a brief account of the long-standing debate over the "two Noras": the charming, manipulative, playacting child-wife and—in a vile phrase—the "fresh-baked suffragette" (Høst, in Paul 195). Many critics have blamed the performers for the split: Hardwick says the tendency has been to play Nora too "lightly" at the outset, too "heavily" at the end (50). Only the exceptional actress, like Tore Segelcke, seems to have achieved the desired synthesis of the two phases of Nora (Noreng 115). Students will have a chance to emulate the perceptiveness of the critics in detecting prior clues to Nora's revolt—her cherished secret life, her pride of accomplishment, her desire to shock her husband—as well as earlier signs of maturity and moral courage, such as her generosity, economic initiative, the forgery itself. They will note Nora's awareness of her husband's failings (act 2) and give due weight to her preference for the company of Dr. Rank; her "unconscious love" of Rank (Noreng 116) may betoken a deep desire for what she calls in her parting line "a true marriage."

The portrayal of Nora offers excellent opportunities for showing how Ibsen has exploited both the resources of poetic language—in particular the poison metaphor—and the so-called poetry of the theater (Northam, *Ibsen's Dramatic Method*, 15–39). In fact, in *A Doll's House* one modulates into the other, since the poison image is enacted in the tarantella. (Students should be encouraged to read up on the folklore belief concerning the tarantula spider, whose effects were thought to include madness and death.) The tarantella can be seen as an "action-symbol which fuses . . . all the various 'parts' of Nora, all the different visions of her" (Ewbank 120); it is a choreographic epiphany of Nora's conflict. For Nora, the dance functions—as it does in the plot—as delaying action; it is also her most flamboyant piece of playacting to hold together the "womanly woman" (to use Shaw's term in *Quintessence*) and the subjectively doomed romantic heroine. As the "womanly" woman, Nora is still acting like Torvald's less than human pet who lives by performing "tricks" for him. Critics, however, have seen her wild abandon during the rehearsal (act 2) as an unconscious expression of her subsequently declared revolt (Heiströvers 102), and the excessive "naturalness" of her performance (act 3) as a presage of her breaking out of a demeaning role (H. Meyer 52). Another critic says that the dance saves Nora from madness and helps to ripen her humanity (Haakonsen, "Das Tarantella-Motiv," in Paul 206–07). The tragic potentiality of the tarantella derives from its folklore conception, according to which it may be a dance of death or a dance of healing: Nora is suspended between life and death. But, instead of Nora, it is her roles—charming pet and willing sacrifice—that go under. As a whole, the dance presents a theatrically effective symbolic action through which the reader or spectator intuitively perceives a change taking place within Nora that will be clearly understood only in act 3.

A certain mythic-religious tinge to Ibsen's language invites a search for deeper meanings. How far one decides to go will depend on the level of the class and the time at one's disposal. Hofmannsthal referred to the "fairy-tale element" in Nora's longing for the "miraculous" (McFarlane, *Henrik Ibsen* 134), a reading confirmed by the fact that she seems to have remained in the nursery: Anne-Marie, Nora's nanny, is still with the family. Moreover, Nora's relationship to her husband—an obvious father figure—suggests an Edenic state of childhood innocence, threatened by the devil (Krogstad) and by death (Rank). Thus viewed, the play can be said to offer a "new interpretation of Genesis" (Baruch 382), with the accent on Nora's exit from the male paradise as the beginning of true humanity.

Christianity as a redemptive religion (rather than myth) provides a more penetrating insight into Nora's predicament. In her "passion" phase, Nora comes to envisage her husband as a savior figure; as she looks forward to the "wonderful thing," the "miracle" that will justify her Kierkegaardian leap of faith in saving the life of her husband, her soul is in a "holy state of advent"

(Høst 185). In view of these transcendent expectations, the evil epiphany of Helmer's moral void becomes devastating. Having absolutized the father substitute (Helmer) into a redemptive God figure, Nora experiences the collapse of that absolute as a kind of death and loses faith not only in her husband but also in the Christian religion. This is obvious from her discussion with Torvald in act 3. The "death of God" amid the paraphernalia of the Nativity sharply accents the ironic dimension of what Ibsen himself called a "modern tragedy" (M. Meyer, *Ibsen: Plays* 2:12).

The Danish critic Erik M. Christensen has discovered a possible source for Nora's attitude, thereby making it more plausible. Quoting from a contemporary theological work (1878) published by the Danish bishop H. Martensen, Christensen argues convincingly that Nora's deification of Helmer conforms to the concept of Christian marriage as then preached—a concept whereby "man is woman's head, just as Christ is the head of the congregation" (127). Christensen's discovery anchors Nora's wildly romantic expectations in social fact. It supports a dialectical interpretation of the central conflict in the play, showing how the ethos of the conventional, Christian marriage founders on the rock of capitalistic bourgeois reality.

It is hardly necessary to emphasize the importance of money in the play to a class of American college students; anyone who reads *A Doll's House* will immediately see its relevance as a countertheme to the "wonderful thing," or the miracle. Within the bourgeois context human values, people themselves, become exchange values: Krogstad is exchangeable with Mrs. Linde, Nora's intimately personal value to Torvald depends on her social rating (she would be no good to him as a forger), and Torvald's own morality is almost totally determined by his socioeconomic status (Rieger 52; Heistrüvers 103–08). And when Nora finally rejects her conditioning, she phrases her rejection in terms of commerce: she wants a settlement ("opgjør") with her husband. While the view that Nora's "real problem" is money (Hardwick 50) may seem extreme, those who have stressed this theme (Bentley, "Ibsen"; Bien; Dukore) have a strong case. As Christensen has shown, in *A Doll's House* "the economic realities unmask religion employed as ideology" (131). In the process, Nora's intimate-private world, centered on a secularized salvational Christianity, is destroyed by the "secret, powerful, and ineluctable forces of society" (Northam, "Ibsen's Search," in Fjelde, *Essays* 100). Being left in an existential and social void, Nora rejects economic support from her husband as well as God and church and initiates her search for self from ground zero.

One of the problems in teaching *A Doll's House* is the difference in dramatic vitality and stage presence between Nora and the other characters. Only an occasional critic has stated that Nora and Helmer are "equally matched" (Valency 156). Most have found Helmer to be an extremely weak antagonist; he has even been called a "caricature" (Gray 55), though Ibsen clearly did not conceive him as such. When he progressively darkened Helmer, his intention was to give Nora a "fighting chance" (Sprinchorn, "Ibsen and the Actors" 121). Ibsen knew that his audience would side with Helmer, causing a "loss of sympathy" for Nora. His expectation is confirmed by a contemporary reviewer who described Helmer as such a "congenial, refined, professionally energetic and honest, domestically happy and likable personality that his greatest offence seems to be that he has chosen a frivolous little girl as his wife" (Marker and Marker 86). My students, however, have shown a very negative response to Helmer. But viewed in the light of bourgeois attitudes and the prevailing patriarchal marriage (which the instructor might explain), he will seem less of an ogre. Moreover, Sprinchorn has noted some positive traits, including his "dramatic self-recognition," which goes "virtually unnoticed because all eyes are on Nora" ("Ibsen and the Actors" 122). If the teacher could establish Torvald's image as being a notch above the common run of bourgeois husbands, the central conflict would gain in verisimilitude and in dramatic excitement.

The discussion of the minor figures could be guided by the question whether they are nothing but plot conveniences or whether Ibsen transcends the merely functional in his treatment of them. It may be noted that even the maid, Anne-Marie, is not just a stock character but introduces a sort of parallel to Nora's final situation: "betrayed" by her lover, Anne-Marie had to abandon her child for economic reasons, just as Nora, after feeling "betrayed" by her husband, abandons her children. Rank is more than "the pawn of an idea" (Bentley, "Ibsen" 345) or a foil to Helmer. While he is necessary to the progress of Nora's "sentimental education"—chiefly by representing what she envisages as a real existential possibility for herself (Lucas 139), just as Krogstad comes to mirror a frightening moral possibility—Doctor Rank's destiny is uniquely his own. Conceived ironically in relation to his profession and helpless in remedying his own illness, he is yet able to meet a ghastly death with courage, even a certain bravado, aware of a secret understanding between himself and Nora. And Krogstad is not a villain in the eyes of my students. They understand that he has been "hard-driven" (Lucas 136) and that the extremes he is prepared to employ to retain his job in the bank have a laudable human motive, namely, to give a good example to his growing boys. Moreover, Krogstad's moral fall was in large part due to Kristine's "betrayal," which caused the "firm ground" to slip away from under his feet (act 3). He is as much a victim of socioeconomic forces as Nora.

The subtlety and complexity of the character relationships in Ibsen's plays are worthy of special study. Of particular interest are the three-way scenes, in which usually two characters communicate—though imperfectly—while the third is ironically unaware of the deeper meaning of what is taking place. An excellent example is provided by the conversation among Nora, Helmer, and Rank in act 3. In this scene, which illustrates the double—or multiple —resonance of Ibsen's language, dialogue becomes gesture: the characters hide as much as they reveal. To each of the three, the moments they spend together mean something intimately individual, though the depth of under- standing varies: Helmer grasps little, Rank more, Nora most of all. With Ibsen's help, the reader or spectator is able to see beyond them all. (The final exchanges in *Hedda Gabler* follow basically the same pattern, though there are four characters on stage.) Such scenes offer excellent opportunities for textual explication through close reading.

In general, the interlocking character relationships in *A Doll's House*—as well as the interrelations between the main plot and the subplots—constitute good topics for student papers. The more ambitious members of the class may accept the challenge of comparing the character constellation in *A Doll's House* with that in *Hedda Gabler*, or Nora with Hedda—called by F. L. Lucas a "doll turned monster" (240)—subjects that have been brilliantly examined by the American critic Arthur Ganz. For practice in argumenta- tion, the students might review, and rebut, one of several critical appraisals, such as those of Hermann Weigand and Ronald Gray, which to most readers will seem idiosyncratic or prejudiced. Weigand sees *A Doll's House* as "sublime" comedy and calls Nora a "bewitching piece of femininity" who, in act 3, enjoys the "greatest moment of her life" (58, 64). Gray's attempt to reduce Ibsen's stature as a dramatist focuses on the play's alleged melodrama and on elements of caricature and the grotesque considered detrimental to Ib- sen's character portrayal (41–58).

For optimum success in teaching *A Doll's House*, the instructor must find not only a fair translation but a sensibly edited text. Rather than an introduc- tory critical essay, which can discourage students from critical ventures of their own, the edition ought to present some relevant biographical-historical material. There exists an abundance of information (including a lengthy monograph about the play by Einar Østvedt) on the genesis of *A Doll's House*, the possible models used for the characters, Ibsen's views on women and women's rights, and the nature of his creative process. If the students had ready access to such information, the class time could be devoted almost exclusively to an understanding of the text. The Michael Meyer text, which I shall be using next time I teach the course, is exemplary in this respect.

A Doll's House has proved extremely successful in introducing honors freshmen at a technological university to dramatic literature, specifically modern tragedy. Through its hierarchy of interwoven themes—bourgeois marriage, women's equality, religion versus materialism, dream versus real- ity—the play elicits a vivid sense of recognition and makes Ibsen our contemporary. For all its well-made features, *A Doll's House* presents a compelling image of human beings confronted by crisis. Perceiving and analyzing the many tragic conflicts in the play—interpersonal, socioeconomic, spiritual—provides the student with a rich aesthetic and intellectual experience.

A *Doll's House* in a Community College

Joanne Gray Kashdan

Golden West College (GWC) is a public community college located in Huntington Beach, Orange County, Southern California. It is part of the Coast Community College District. By law, GWC has an open-door admissions policy: any high school graduate or anyone over eighteen years of age is eligible to attend; with special permission, high school seniors may also attend. As of this writing, no tuition is charged. GWC opened in 1966, providing the first two years of transferable liberal arts education, remedial services, vocational education, and community services. The academic calendar follows the semester system, with both day and evening instruction. GWC serves nearly 20,000 students a semester, about 15,000 of whom are part-time students. Some 12,500 attend day classes, and roughly 7,000 attend evening classes. The average age of students is twenty-four to twenty-five, although my own students have ranged from sixteen to sixty-seven. My experience is based on these student demographics.

At GWC, I teach—among other courses—English 110, at night. Maximum enrollment is thirty-five students. The class meets once a week for three hours. Ibsen's *A Doll's House* is part of that course, which is described in the college catalog as follows:

> ENGLISH 110: Introduction to Literature: Composition
> Prerequisite: English 100 (Freshman Comp.)
> An introduction to literature and further study of composition, emphasizing critical analysis and evaluation of fiction, poetry, and drama. Recommended for English majors and prospective teachers. Satisfies general education requirement.

The diversity of the course makes concentration on any single work of literature impossible. *A Doll's House* thus occupies one three-hour class meeting.

For a text, I use an anthology, *Literature: The Human Experience* (ed. Abcarian and Klotz). Generally, I like the anthology for its international scope; specifically, I find Otto Reinert's translation of *A Doll's House* authentic and useful, for it is accurate (within my limited reading of Norwegian, supplemented by the advice of a colleague who is fluent in Norwegian), and it is presented in current, idiomatic American English. Another benefit of this textbook is that it includes Doris Lessing's short story "To Room Nineteen," which deals with issues ancillary to *A Doll's House*. Therefore, I assign Lessing's story before assigning Ibsen's play.

In my course presentation, I divide the material into three segments, according to genre (approximately six weeks each). I emphasize a different critical approach with each genre. The first segment is poetry, with a formalist approach. (Less capable and less diligent students—usually about eight to ten—are scared off and drop out at this point.) Next, I present short stories with a sociological approach. (Students who cannot manage an interdisciplinary attitude—about seven—now depart.) Finally, I address drama with a psychological approach—Freud, Jung, Gestalt, behaviorist, existential, and abnormal. I have a six-page handout describing these approaches. (By now, I am down to eighteen to twenty serious students and can engage in genuinely analytical work.) In the drama segment, in which assignments are structurally the same as those for the other two segments, I require a paper applying psychological criticism to a play not assigned for classroom discussion. I also require an essay examination on the four plays that are assigned: *Antigone, Othello, A Doll's House,* and *The Glass Menagerie.* The exam consists of eight questions—two on each of the plays—from which students choose two.

For *A Doll's House,* the questions are:

> You are a psychologist specializing in abnormal psychology. Torvald Helmer comes to you and says: "My dear doctor, it appears to me that my wife Nora has betrayed me not just with Krogstad (the swine) and Dr. Rank (who might be permitted other follies) but also with more important matters that involve finance, forgery, and banking. I believe she must be quite ill, mentally speaking, and must be institutionalized for her own good." What do you tell Torvald? Why?

> You are a Gestalt psychologist. Nora Helmer comes to you and says: "My life is quite fragmented. With my husband Torvald, with Krogstad, even with Dr. Rank and Mrs. Linde, I must play a role, but that role is not the real *me.* I know who I am. But I cannot be myself with others. Please help me." How do you advise Nora? Why?

Classroom presentation of *A Doll's House* is another matter. Given my student demographics, I find that much historical background is needed to make *A Doll's House* comprehensible. Fortunately, in 1975 I wrote a critical article to accompany the plot summary of *A Doll's House* for *Masterplots,* revised edition (ed. Frank N. Magill). The article gave me an opportunity to crystallize my ideas about *A Doll's House.*

In that article, I point out that *Et dukkehjem* had a twofold impact: in dramaturgy and in sociology. In 1879 Ibsen broke through the dramaturgical milieu of historical romances and comedies of manners to establish realistic drama as a legitimate art form, a form that continues to the present. Further,

I note that Ibsen addressed and legitimated social problems as a serious concern of modern theater. I also describe social attitudes of the late nineteenth century, with special reference to the legal and social status of women. Additionally, I have written, for the same publication, critical articles on other plays by Ibsen: *Brand, Peer Gynt, Hedda Gabler, Ghosts,* and *Rosmersholm.* The interested instructor may wish to consult this material, which I use extensively in my classroom presentations.

I find the presentation of biographical information about Ibsen very important, and I recommend that instructors study at least two or three books on Ibsen's life: Halvdan Koht's *Life of Ibsen,* Adolf E. Zucker's anecdotal *Ibsen: The Master Builder,* and Michael Meyer's useful and reliable *Ibsen.* For critical works, I recommend avoiding any of George Bernard Shaw's seductive comments on Ibsen, since they are biased by Shaw's socialism, with which Ibsen was not sympathetic.

Hermann J. Weigand's *The Modern Ibsen* and Otto Heller's *Henrik Ibsen: Plays and Problems* are helpful. But the best, I think, is William Archer's introduction to his translation of Ibsen's works, which includes, in the last volume, a biography by Edmund Gosse. Brian Downs, *Ibsen: The Intellectual Background,* is good on Ibsen's early work. Other useful sources are Storm Jameson's *Modern Drama in Europe* and Eric Bentley's *The Playwright as Thinker.* I synthesize these works for classroom lectures, inasmuch as my students would be intimidated by formal requirements to read them.

Among supplementary materials, I refer to Doris Lessing's short story "To Room Nineteen." I also refer to the 1980 film *Kramer vs. Kramer* (an obvious analogy) and the 1981 film *First Monday in October* (analogy and contrast) as well as the two film versions of Ibsen's *A Doll's House,* both 1973 releases, one starring Claire Bloom and the other starring Jane Fonda. Most important, I present Claire Boothe Luce's *A Doll's House 1970 (With Apologies to Henrik Ibsen).* The Luce update reminds students that the social problem enunciated in Ibsen's play is not antiquated. I read Luce's one-act play—without preliminaries—in class. The reading takes thirty or forty minutes, at most. Luce is a surprise and a bonus, for students respond to the real drama of the Luce play spontaneously—as though it were a real performance. Consequently, they make the connection between Ibsen and Luce, and I can span one hundred years relatively effortlessly. In fact, a year ago, after I had thus broached *A Doll's House* to my class, one of my women students (about 35 years old) exclaimed: "When I read this play, I realized I had been married to Torvald for seven years before I divorced him!" A valuable source on this issue is Eugene R. August's article " 'Modern Men'; or, Men's Studies in the '80's." Classroom discussion is lively, sometimes heated.

A further stimulus to classroom discussion is the matter of language, specifically translation. Students understand that Torvald uses derogatory diminutives to address Nora: "Lerkefuglen" is "lark"; "ekornet" is "squirrel"; "lille spillefuglen" is "little wastrel"; "lille sanglerken" is "little songbird." In addition, the closing stage directions—"nedenfra høres drønnet av en port som slås i lås" 'the door [port] slams/bangs [slås] into the lock [lås]'—convey, in Norwegian, much more than they do in English. Students are impressed by such fine points of language, so long as those points of language do not appear formidable or do not overwhelm them. (My source is Henrik Ibsen, *Nutidsdramaer, 1877–99.*)

The most volatile concerns for my students, however, are the social issues embedded in the play. The classroom atmosphere is relaxed; thus students feel free to ask questions and to challenge the "givens" of literary, sociological, and psychological interpretations. I find myself in the uncomfortable position of being referee: my women students identify simplistically with Nora; my men students identify likewise with Torvald. I remind them that Ibsen, in his original version, designated speaking parts with "Nora" (first name) and "Helmer" (last name)—now an obvious sexist ploy. Still, I emphasize that Ibsen was not a partisan but a realist, reflecting the values of his time. I must caution my students to observe civilized behavior.

Amid the controlled chaos, I try to stress that *A Doll's House* is important in the evolution of dramaturgy. Nonetheless, my students compel me to view the play as sociology. All the while, we are trying to analyze the play psychologically. These competing forces produce a vivacious and contentious three hours of class meeting, but it is all educational because education takes place when ideas are matched against other ideas.

Lastly, in this electronically wired age, I have utilized three devices to pedagogical advantage. First, I recommend cable and subscription television services to my students as supplements to classroom materials. Second, I suggest VCR tapes—both Beta and VHS formats are available in this area at quite reasonable rental prices—of supplementary materials such as films (*Kramer vs. Kramer, First Monday in October*). Finally, I have learned to live with audiocassette recorders. My students often tape my lectures. When they do, I borrow the tapes and have the GWC audiovisual services dub the students' tapes onto my own blanks; then, at home, I listen to what I have done. My *Doll's House* lecture has been both a humbling and an instructive experience. I learned that my strengths were with the drama itself and that I tended to be overbearing in classroom discussion. Subsequently, I have modified my conduct during those discussions and produced much more satisfactory results.

I have been extraordinarily blessed with fundamentally good students and the freedom to explore scholarly avenues. The result is an undergraduate second-semester freshman course with the latitude—and the occasional exhilaration—usually associated with a more advanced course.

COURSES IN DRAMATIC LITERATURE

Teaching *A Doll's House*: An Outline

Otto Reinert

In a course with time for only one Ibsen play, *A Doll's House* is as good a choice as any. In theme and dramaturgy it adequately represents Ibsen's late and most significant drama: the twelve prose plays he wrote between 1877 and 1899. Of them all, it is the breakthrough play of modern dramatic realism. It has two additional advantages. A play of no extraordinary subtlety, it is more accessible to students than some of the others. Since that doesn't keep it from being one of the most misunderstood of all Ibsen's plays, there is an extra edge to the challenge of teaching it.

How it is taught obviously depends on the course. I assume here that I am teaching the play in an upper-division, undergraduate drama course for literature majors who already have some idea of what drama is. I use my own translation (Reinert and Arnott). In my ten-week course I allot three class hours to *A Doll's House*. I don't have my students act out scenes and rarely use videotapes or records of film and stage performances.

Rather than three lectures on the play or a complete scenario of classroom dialogues, I have put together an agenda of facts, topics, issues, viewpoints, and insights that I think students should know about. I have neither the presumption nor the space to offer actual and prospective teachers of Ibsen *my* prose for *their* students. I suggest topics to cover and points to make and in what sequence. Some things I have included because students have asked questions and raised points about them. Other students will ask other questions and make other points. I refer (in parenthesis) to works I have found useful in my own thinking about *A Doll's House* or that deal at some length with what I can do little more than mention here. The references are keyed to the list of works cited at the end of the volume.

In my classroom experience with *A Doll's House*, the main problem has been to keep students who have been raised on social revolution and consciousness-raising from running away with the play into discussion of social issues in general and feminism in particular. When they do, they lose the ambivalent tragedy Ibsen wrote: Nora Helmer's painful and degrading discovery of what male society has made of her. The artistic and intellectual strength of the play is Ibsen's virtually seamless joining of a thesis play to a traditional tragedy of inner waste. The tragedy invests the thesis with emotive power, the thesis the tragedy with continuing relevance.

Day 1: Background

Biography. Ibsen's father lost his business when Ibsen was seven. At eighteen, Ibsen fathered an illegitimate child (Koht 29, 38; M. Meyer, *Biography* 12–14, 31–32; all subsequent page refs. to Meyer are to the *Biography*). Financial ruin, loss of social status, illegitimacy are recurrent motifs in Ibsen's plays, including *A Doll's House*.

Apprenticeship as manager of theaters in Bergen and Christiania (now Oslo) in the late 1850s and early 1860s (Koht 70–133; M. Meyer 84–194). Apparent lack of interest in theater in later life: rarely attended rehearsals and performances, would not let his plays be produced before publication, referred to them as "books," only occasional letters to directors with suggestions for casting and staging (M. Meyer 274, 538, 568–69, 721). (Contrast Shakespeare, Molière.)

Disillusionment when Norway (and Sweden, then in political union with Norway) failed to come to Denmark's aid in the Dano-Prussian War of 1863. Loss of faith in pan-Scandinavianism. Contempt for Norwegians and Norwegian nationalism (Koht 169–77; M. Meyer 212–15, 222).

Voluntary exile in Italy and Germany from 1864 till 1891. Said he needed geographical distance to write about life in Norway (M. Meyer 517).

Vowed to become a "photographer" after critical rejection of *Peer Gynt* (1867)—to leave poetic vision in verse for social fact in prose. Beginning in 1877, he did so—in form, not in substance (Koht 242; M. Meyer 270).

Source. Story of wife who forges a bond without her husband's knowledge in order to save his life is based on a disastrous episode in the life of Laura Kieler, a young Norwegian author, whom Ibsen knew personally (Koht 314–15, 318–19, 460; M. Meyer 443–45, 634–35, 680).

General source for all the problem plays: the Danish critic Georg Brandes's *Hovedstrømminger i det 19de Aarhundredes Literatur* (1872). A main point: "Modern literature proves its viability by submitting problems to debate" (trans. mine). Ibsen, who rarely acknowledged indebtedness to anyone, wrote Brandes about the seminal impact his book had had on him (Koht 279–81; M. Meyer 356–59; Sprinchorn, *Letters* 120–23).

Place in the Canon. A Doll's House (1879) is one of Ibsen's social problem plays. The others: *Pillars of Society* (1877), *Ghosts* (1881), *An Enemy of the People* (1882). Business and politics are the areas of conflict in the plays with male protagonists (*Pillars, Enemy*); the "woman" plays (*Doll's House, Ghosts*) are about family relationships. *A Doll's House* and *Ghosts* are complementary: in one, the wife leaves; in the other, she stays—with consequences far more grim. Both are naturalistic: characters are the victims of their biological heredity and social conditioning (Dr. Rank's "rotting spine" becomes Oswald Alving's syphilis).

Social problem play: a particular instance of a general condition. Individual as victim, society as victimizer. Dialogue on rightness or wrongness of social institutions, conventions, attitudes. Action "proves" that, given certain characters in certain circumstances, prevailing social forms have distressful consequences (Fergusson, *Idea* 146–52). Three indispensable ingredients: truthfulness to the realities of contemporary middle-class life, controversial meaning, tight and exciting plot—realism, topicality, suspense. The formula made Ibsen "the father" of a drama that quickly superseded farce, melodrama, pseudo-Shakespeare. Tentative predecessors: Hebbel, Scribe, Augier, Dumas fils, Tom Robertson (Gassner 335–83). Ibsen's superiority: liberalism more daring and cogent, moral fervor stronger, constructions subtler and clearer, characterization more penetrating, dramatic imagination altogether finer.

Ibsen's early plays: saga and ballad plays, Roman histories, romantic satires. Most important: *Brand* (1866), *Peer Gynt* (1867)—large, complementary, mythopoeic verse dramas of ambiguous outcome on (respectively) excess and deficiency of will and on moral and metaphysical meaning of true selfhood. It is arguable that Ibsen never transcended the dialectic of autonomous individualism and traditional authority–social obligation in this great dramatic dyad (Bentley, *Playwright* 30–32, 76–90): selfhood—what it is, how won, its cost to self and others—is the central theme in all the later plays.

After social-problem plays, Ibsen's dramatic conflicts seem more "psychological" (protagonist self-divided) than "social," but this subtle, gradual shift should not be exaggerated. Nora and Mrs. Alving are "psychological" heroines facing personal dilemmas for which there is no "social" resolution.

Reception. Intense controversy wherever *A Doll's House* was staged and read, pitting conservatives (sanctity of marriage and motherhood) against liberals (individual's right to seek selfhood on her or his own terms) (Koht 320–23; M. Meyer 454–58). A contemporary journalist: "When Nora slammed the door shut on her marriage, walls shook in a thousand homes." Since copyright laws gave Ibsen no control over his plays outside of Scandinavia, he reluctantly changed the ending to satisfy a German actress who refused to play Nora unless she stayed with her children (Koht 321; M. Meyer 459).

Ibsen's Theater. Developed from seventeeth-century French baroque theater. Spectators, in darkness, look into lighted, box-like stage, framed by proscenium arch, the "missing" fourth wall in the family living room. Physical and psychological distance between stage and audience favors illusionism. Audience peeks and eavesdrops on lives of persons unaware of being watched and listened to. Authentic sets, props, costumes; natural acting style (Duke of Saxe-Meiningen's company; later, Stanislavsky at Moscow Art Theater). Technological innovations during Ibsen's lifetime: electric light for gas, revolving stage (Brockett, chs. 15, 16). Realism compatible with symbolism, as in Ibsen's cluttered, "inhibiting" interiors (Northam, *Ibsen's Dramatic Method* 11–39).

Realism didn't abolish stage conventions. For verse, soliloquy, aside, and so on, it substituted a larger, more basic convention: there is no audience; the stage is not a stage but some other place.

The World of Ibsen's Plays. Identity crisis in nineteenth-century bourgeois society. Social, political, economic structures changing, disintegrating, under assault of continuous revolutions. Secularization, democratization, industrialization, urbanization. Religion versus science, philosophical positivism (Comte) and materialism (Marx) versus idealism (Kant, Hegel, Kierkegaard). Expanding free-enterprise capitalism trying uneasily to accommodate itself to traditional hierarchies and to orthodox Christian ethos of meekness, altruism, priority of spirit over matter, revelation over empiricism. Ibsen's protagonists typically caught in tension among conflicting values, ideologies (Downs, *Ibsen*; Johnston, *Ibsen*). To Shaw, Ibsen was primarily the liberal, truth-telling iconoclast, knocking down false ideals.

Day 2: Form and Technique

Retrospectiveness. Story (as distinct from *plot*) virtually over by the time play begins; only the catastrophe remains to be enacted. "Drama of ripe condition": situation charged from beginning, though no one knows it; dialogue a progressive unlayering of the past. Drama of exposure: the hidden secret shattering the complacent surface (Brustein, *Theatre* 66). Classical paradigm: *Oedipus Rex* (Mrs. Linde as "Messenger from Corinth," whose arrival innocently triggers catastrophe). Intellectual premise: law of causality. Ethical corollary: we are what we have and have not done and what has and has not been done to us. The Helmer marriage destroyed not just by Nora's forgery but by her whole conditioning from girlhood on by a society run by men. Ghosts are in *A Doll's House* as in *Ghosts*.

Exposition by Innuendo. The technical trick in retrospective realism is to convey to the audience vital information about the past in plausible, apparently inconsequential talk. Device: exposition that is continual, fragmentary, inferential. A fine example in *A Doll's House*: Helmer's failing to indict Nora's father because he had fallen in love with his daughter.

Well-madeness. The intricate weaving together of plot events in a compact, suspenseful plot of "strong" (theatrically effective) scenes. Derogatory connotations of all carpentry, no content. But Ibsen's well-madeness is on the whole credible and functional: the old relationship between villain and confidante; the many interlocking money motifs; Christmas season ironically coinciding with destruction of the happy home; juxtaposition of the two man-woman confrontations in act 3; the timing of Krogstad's two entrances in act 1: the first to coincide with Mrs. Linde's first visit and with Nora's expression of joy in her new freedom from money worries, the second to interrupt with "business" from men's "serious" and "adult" world Nora's game of hide-and-seek with her children. In comparison, Mrs. Linde's explanation in act 3 of why she and Krogstad have to meet and talk in the Helmers' living room seems contrived—a piece of awkward well-madeness forced on Ibsen by his need for keeping his setting single.

Structure. The structure of *A Doll's House* comes close to observing the neoclassical three unities. Only the subplot and the three-day time span do not conform to the strictest interpretation of the unities of action and time.

Plot links: after Krogstad's first threat, Nora knows she lives on borrowed time before the terrible-wonderful testing of her marriage, and Krogstad's letter (and the mailbox) becomes a focus for suspense; by not letting Krogstad ask for his letter back, Mrs. Linde takes it on herself to force the Helmers to clarification. Two peripeties: in act 1, Nora's euphoria becomes fear, doubt, guilt; in act 3, Krogstad's second letter does not fulfill its promise of happy ending.

Final scene changes mode of play from fast-paced melodrama (blackmailer's reform, etc.) to scenically static debate. Is play's unity compromised? Not if we discern the "true" Nora in her frustration and resentment in early scenes (overtipping, macaroon business, conscious play-acting, touchiness about being patronized, pride in her secret, impulse to say "damn!" in Helmer's hearing).

Character Configuration. The two couples as mutual and ironic foils: moving in opposite directions, their relative position at the end a reversal of what it was at first. Leaving, Nora faces a future that in its emotional desolation and economic uncertainty repeats Mrs. Linde's and the nurse's in the past.

Dr. Rank is the only major character not essential to the plot. His function, therefore, may not seem clear. Points to consider: his Darwinian impatience (in act 1) with society's coddling moral invalids; his physical and Nora's moral inheritance from a corrupt father (and Nora's potential corruption of *her* children); his embodying Nora's fantasy wealthy admirer; the way this decent, intelligent man's selfless love for Nora certifies her worth *before* she reveals her true integrity and depth at the end; the irony that the only man Nora has ever been able really to talk to never learns her secret; the subtle ambiguities in Nora's motivation in their silk stocking scene (act 2); his dying coinciding with the end of his best friends' marriage; his self-sought isolation paralleling Nora's.

Imagery. Life in Helmer home defined by three off-stage institutions: bank, nursery, hospital. Other images: Nora's hiding things (Christmas tree, macaroons, the loan, herself), wanting to "tear things to pieces" (bond, costume, herself).

Symbolism. Imagery tends to take on symbolic power, as facts, acts, objects, words of ordinary domesticity get charged with larger meanings. Obvious examples: Helmer's pet animal names for Nora, her petty lying and deliberate seductiveness, money exchanged for love (both Helmer and Rank), children's games, stripped Christmas tree, black clothing (Rank's "invisibility hat," Helmer's black domino that Nora puts on), the tarantella dance (working off tension, last fling at life), the "light" Nora offers Rank in his last scene and his thanking her for it, the doffed masquerade costume, the closed door to Helmer's study behind which he reads Krogstad's letter.

Language. Speech is the everyday speech of educated middle-class people. Language is economical, pregnant—not because all speeches are short and crisp, but because hardly any speech includes words that don't contribute to the drama. Rare heightened speech—Helmer's drunken amorousness, Nora's broken soliloquy as she is about to go out and kill herself—points up crucially defining emotions. Sacrifice of one kind of "poetry" for another. Ibsen's language in dialogue is more than just authentic realism, but it works because it is that, too (Ewbank 120–21).

Day 3: Thesis and Tragedy

Ibsen's Preliminary "Notes for the Modern Tragedy"

> There are two kinds of spiritual law, two kinds of conscience: one is man's, the other, quite different, is woman's. They do not understand one another, but in practical life woman is judged by man's law, as if she were not a woman, but a man.
>
> At the end, the wife in the play feels trapped, doesn't know what is right and wrong. The conflict between her natural feeling and her faith in authority confuses her.

A woman cannot be herself in today's society, . . .

. . . .
. . . She must bear it all alone. The catastrophe approaches, re-
morselessly, inevitably. Despair, struggle, and ruin.   (19 Oct. 1878;
qtd. in Koht 315–16; M. Meyer 446)

These don't sound like notes for a play about a feminist heroine—strong,
militant, triumphant, sure of what she wants and what she stands for. *A
Doll's House* is not a play about that kind of heroine.

Beyond Feminism. On the occasion of Ibsen's seventieth birthday, in 1898,
the Norwegian Association for Women's Rights gave a dinner in his honor.
To their toast to "the creator of Nora" Ibsen replied:

> . . . I have been more of a poet and less of a social philosopher than
> most people have been inclined to believe. I am grateful for your toast,
> but I can't claim the honor of ever having worked consciously for
> women's rights. I'm not even sure I know what they are. To me it has
> seemed a matter of human rights.   (Koht 455; M. Meyer 774–75;
> Sprinchorn, *Letters* 337–38)

There is no contradiction between his speech and his notes of twenty years
before. Nora is society's victim because her husband and the patriarchal
society he represents denies her her *human* rights as *a woman*.

Thesis. On the issue between Nora and society: either she is as ignorant,
immature, and irresponsible as Helmer says she is, or she is right in breaking
a law that will not let her spare her dying father anguish and save her
husband's life. In one case, society stands charged with not educating its
women for "real" life; in the other, with failing to change its laws to accommodate woman's conscience. In either case, Nora is "right," society "wrong."
The male establishment is in a double bind, the problem play "proving" a
social evil.

Tragedy. But thesis is not play; Nora's triumph is tainted. She is no more
the unequivocal "heroine" than Helmer is the unequivocal "villain." To
assume that such was Ibsen's intention is to have difficulties reconciling it
with the actual characters: Nora, selfish and silly, slyly manipulative, a romantic sentimentalist; Helmer, successful, protective, intelligent, with taste
and wit and charm, affectionate, ardent lover, a "good" husband (Weigand
26–75).

Helmer *is* a good husband by conventional standards. Nora *is* naive, possibly a less than ideal mother, certainly prostituted in her role as his helpless,
adorable little plaything. Her final self-assessment is accurate: "Nothing has
become of me." The system that lets men "own" women forces women to
disown themselves. Her eyes opened, all she can see is her doll's-house

existence as stunting, demeaning, trivial, impoverished ("fun" is not happiness). If daughterhood and wifehood have made her a sex object, she has to get out if she is to become a human being. Her tragedy: her exit is an act of uncertain outcome and questionable morality that costs her her home and family. She leaves her children in the hands of a man she no longer respects, and she is deaf to his new contriteness and plea for a second chance. Nothing he says penetrates her devastating realization that "the wonderful"—or "the miracle"—("det vidunderlige") she was waiting for in ecstasy and terror—the proof that Torvald's love for her was capable of a sacrifice equal to hers for him—has been nothing but illusion. *That* she cannot forgive him, or his share in making her what she now despises herself for being: a confused, frightened, loveless woman-yet-to-be.

Nora's self-recognition and her leaving are neither "right" nor "wrong"—just inevitable, difficult, sad, another instance in Ibsen's drama of the high cost of selfhood. Ibsen's case is stronger, not weaker, if we don't let the tragedy disappear in polemics about women's rights. *A Doll's House* is neither a partisan nor an obsolete play.

How to Get into *A Doll House*: Ibsen's Play as an Introduction to Drama

June Schlueter

As a student and teacher of modern and contemporary drama, I have often heard colleagues scoff over the corpse of Ibsen, admitting Ibsen's seminal position in the development of modern drama but concluding that from the vantage point of the 1980s, the only proper place for an Ibsen play is the morgue. When I read Peter Handke or Sam Shepard, I feel inclined to agree, but come fall, and the first half of the modern drama course I teach, I am once again surprised at the continuing vitality of Ibsen's plays. And I am excited by the range of effective approaches to teaching them.

A Doll House, in particular, offers such accessible riches for undergraduates that it has remained a favorite of both of ours. I continue to teach the play, not only because it holds so important a place in literary history or because the issues of individualism and women's choices are anything but dead but because it offers the best initiation into drama I know. In my modern drama classes as well as my introductory literature classes, I suggest three ways of getting into *A Doll House*: the first through the front door, the second through the back door, and the third through the chimney.

The front door, of course, is the door Nora slams, and strictly speaking, it is the door that ends the play, though not for students: the temptation to speculate about what happens to Nora after she slams the door is simply too appealing. Predictably, they speak of the difficulties facing women in the nineteenth century, of the fragility of Nora's personality, of how ill-equipped she is to make it on her own. Some argue, however, that she has just demonstrated how capable and independent she is and that despite the odds set by society her chances of survival are high. Before the discussion has gone too far, I share with them my own somewhat imperfect recollection of "To Norway—Land of the Giants," the delightful Monty Python scenarios, each only several seconds long, of what happens to Nora. In one, a group of suffragettes marching by just as she exits tramples her; in another, she slips on the icy stairs and slides headfirst into an open manhole; in a third, she opens her umbrella and is next seen flying above the rooftops, Mary Poppins style; and in a fourth, my favorite, Nora does not really intend to leave after all but is simply playacting again: she hides behind the door as Torvald charges after her, pushing against the door and flattening her against the wall. Since *A Doll House* is the first play of the course, the Python skits prove a great icebreaker and an effective way of suggesting how fatuous an endeavor such speculation is. The play, after all, has ended, and Nora has no life beyond it.

What I am doing here, of course, is introducing students to the limits of literary criticism. If we are not justified in speaking of Nora's postplay existence, are we in speaking of her preplay existence? I tell them of the Jane Fonda film version of *A Doll House*, which spends the first twenty minutes on material that precedes the opening scene of the text. But Nora and Torvald's trip to Italy, her father's death, her arrangement with Krogstad are not speculation: all are revealed in the text, but through exposition rather than dramatization. We deviate for a few moments then and look at how Ibsen uses the uncomplicated but certain technique of the old school chum's return so that Nora might plausibly reveal the facts of her recent past, which will prove essential to the development of the plot.

Once students understand the boundaries of a play, we can then move on to the limitations prescribed by the text. We cannot, for example, infer from Nora's forgery that the money was not obtained from her father at all but from a lover, though we might be justified in speculating a bit about Nora's relationship with Dr. Rank. Students are eager to suggest possibilities and have others decide how responsible those readings are. Inevitably, they come to see the legitimacy of variant readings: one student might see love as Nora's motivation for concealing the forgery from Torvald, another might see egotism, a third moral carelessness. I move then to the macaroon scenes and ask how those scenes support each of the interpretations.

In the first of these two early scenes, Nora has been surreptitiously devouring the forbidden macaroons. When Torvald asks whether his little "sweet tooth" has been breaking rules, she denies that she has. He becomes more specific and asks whether she "didn't drop in at the confectioner's." "No, I assure you, Torvald—," she replies. "She didn't nibble a little candy?" "No, really not." "Not even a macaroon or two?" "No, Torvald," she retorts, "I assure you—really—," and even after Torvald turns his questions into a joke, she continues to insist, "It would never occur to me to go against your wishes" (Le Gallienne, *Six Plays* 6–7). Is Nora so intent on pleasing her husband that she tells him what she knows he wants to hear? Is she so full of self that she delights in deceiving the imperceptive Torvald? Or is she so morally irresponsible that she will lie whenever lying suits her convenience?

In the second of the scenes, Nora brazenly offers Rank some macaroons and easily lies, saying, in Kristine's presence, that Kristine brought the macaroons. As the three of them eat the cookies, Nora exclaims over her happiness but admits, to Rank's astonishment, that her one wish is to tell Torvald "'damn it all!'" (*Six Plays* 20–21).

Those who saw Nora as the innocent wife, motivated by love of husband, begin to reconsider. By now they are beginning to understand how an interpretation of an individual scene commits them to a particular interpretation of a later scene and, ultimately, to the entire play; if Nora is deceitful and manipulative from the start, as these scenes suggest, then perhaps her leaving reflects only a petulant woman's irresponsibility rather than a maturing vision of self.

The "back door" through which I then enter the play is a back door in the metaphoric sense. This entrance is through a scene that is not in the play, or at least not in the Eva Le Gallienne translation, which I intentionally use. The scene is the silk-stocking scene between Nora and Dr. Rank, present in the original and in every other translation. Le Gallienne's decision to omit it seems an act of charity toward Nora, who has a much more difficult time defending her innocence when it is left in. In the scene, Nora suggestively queries Rank whether a pair of silk stockings will fit her:

> NORA. . . . Doctor Rank, come and sit down here, and I will show you something.
> RANK (*sitting down*). What is it?
> NORA. Just look at those!
> RANK. Silk stockings.
> NORA. Flesh-coloured. Aren't they lovely? It is so dark here now, but to-morrow—. No, no, no! you must only look at the feet. Oh well, you may have leave to look at the legs too.
> RANK. Hm—
> NORA. Why are you looking so critical? Don't you think they will fit me?
> RANK. I have no means of forming an opinion about that.
> NORA (*looks at him for a moment*). For shame! (*Hits him lightly on the ear with the stockings.*) That's to punish you. (*Folds them up again.*)
> RANK. And what other nice things am I to be allowed to see?
> NORA. Not a single thing more, for being so naughty. (*She looks among the things, humming to herself.*) (Sharp 38–39)

Those who thought Nora morally irresponsible earlier are convinced this scene confirms their interpretation. But those who saw Nora as an innocent argue that only one so naive as she could dare to be so reckless. I like to remind students at this point of Torvald's sententious warning against morally corrupt mothers, which at first sounded so silly, and suggest that it might deserve a second look here. Though Torvald knew nothing of the macaroons or the stockings, he still, ironically, identifies the dangers of moral degeneracy to Nora. By going back to Torvald's speech, students can consider the extent to which they should trust the assessment of one character by another.

I now have the opportunity to discuss ways in which a playwright creates character and introduce the students to Alvin Kernan's classic essay in *Char-*

acter and Conflict (7–23). We spend a fair amount of time looking at what other characters—particularly Torvald and Kristine—say about Nora's character and at what Nora's actions and speeches—especially in the traumatic tarantella scene—say about her. In the initial meeting between Nora and Kristine, Kristine speaks of Nora's chronic immaturity, which is enough to prompt Nora to reveal the story of the borrowed funds. The scene proves productive, since students become aware of the subtext that is operating: the moment is not so much the sharing of intimacies by old friends as it is an expression of Nora's egotistical need for an audience: she is both defending her maturity and, by boasting as she does, confirming her immaturity, which has been previously revealed by her insistence on speaking of her own good fortune in the face of Kristine's difficulties.

By now, the little lark has managed to win the students' disapproval on several counts, despite their obvious admiration for her at play's end. This is a perfect moment to talk about complexity of character and about character development and to let the students decide whether the Nora who slams the door on the dollhouse is consistent with the early Nora. Those who insist she has changed may at first think consistency irrelevant, until others remind them of the revealing moments that suggested Nora had the capacity for such independent action from the start.

The cast of complementary characters in *A Doll House* is also worth discussing here, for the Ibsen play, more than any other modern play I know, orchestrates its characters so that they illuminate the protagonist—in much the same way that Shakespeare's *Lear* or Middleton's *The Changeling* creates a subplot with a Gloucester or an Isabella whose actions parallel the actions of Lear or Beatrice-Joanna. Kristine, for example, though somewhat colorless, is a mature, independent woman who for years sacrificed herself for others. Not only does she suggest the potential of Nora, but her former situation suggests that Nora, too, has been involved in self-sacrifice, not in the consciously selfless actions of her school friend but in the relinquishing of her personal identity by playing Torvald's squirrel. Krogstad's situation, of course, also parallels Nora's: in Torvald's judgment, both forgers are moral degenerates, unfit to bring up their children. Similarly, Rank has inherited a physically debilitating disease, just as Nora, according to Torvald, has inherited her father's immoral disposition. As Rank's condition deteriorates, so does Nora's, with Rank announcing plans to be invisible (i.e., dead) at the next masquerade ball just as Nora is planning her suicide. Rank's black-cross calling cards mark not only his imminent death but Nora's (which, of course, does not occur) and the imminent death of the relationship between Nora and her husband as well. Even Anne-Marie's situation parallels Nora's, for she abandoned her child for its own good, just as Nora finally abandons hers.

The third way into *A Doll House*, through the chimney, needs some explanation. For decades, Ibsen has been seen as a realistic social playwright, a believer in the law of causality in dramatic structure. But as Robert Brustein has noted in "The Crack in the Chimney," Ibsen has himself, on occasion, repealed that law. In *The Master Builder*, Solness notices the crack in the chimney flue but does nothing to repair it, knowing it might result in a fire. A fire does indeed destroy the family home and change Solness's personal and professional life. But the crack in the chimney had nothing to do with the fire, which inexplicably began in a closet. We review *A Doll House*, then, with causal construction in mind, noting the dramatic question each scene raises and resolves and charting the movement of the play from point A to point B to point C.

I want students to see that in dramatic terms the ending of *A Doll House* is perfectly appropriate. At a showing of *A Doll House* in a college film series once, a group of older-generation viewers insisted Nora was wrong in leaving her husband and, particularly, her children. I allowed them this judgment but distinguished between moral rightness and dramatic rightness, suggesting that all the action in the play justified Nora's departure. Since many of my students are familiar with *Oedipus Rex* from their high school days, we speak of inexorability, asking whether the same deliberateness of action that characterizes the Greek play is present here. All agree that the sense is stronger in *Oedipus*, noting the inescapable oracle under which Oedipus must operate. Though Oedipus's character and decisions coincide with the prescription of destiny, students feel the power and presence of the edict that will destroy him. In *A Doll House*, by contrast, an early modern play in which moral imperatives may successfully be denied, Nora's choices alone prescribe her fate.

For a fairly long time in act 3, though, Ibsen has us believe that Nora will take the path of the nineteenth-century fallen woman and commit suicide. She discusses this intention with Krogstad and, indirectly, with Rank, and she is headed out the door toward the river when Torvald stops her. Ibsen seems here to be offering alternative endings for his audience: one that a nineteenth-century audience might expect, the other that would shock it. Dramatically, though, either fits the causal construction of the play. Nora's suicide would have confirmed her immaturity, her inability to be honest, her unwillingness to endure the consequences of her actions; it would have meant that her romantic vision of marriage had failed and that she was unable to rearrange her marriage on adult terms. Her previous emotional immaturities, reflected in her games with Torvald, her selfish chatter with Kristine, and the manic tarantella scene, would all come together to confirm the dramatic rightness of the suicide. Nora, however, gets a second chance, but this ending too is dramatically justified, since throughout the play and particularly in her final dialogue with Torvald Nora shows the potential for mature action. Indeed, early productions in England and Germany sanitized the last act by having Nora yield to Torvald's pleas and remain his wife, yet another ending that might be justified in dramatic terms.

There are several moments in the play when the action might have gone one of two or more ways, but none of these moments reveals a crack in the chimney. Krogstad, for example, might have withdrawn the letter, putting Nora in the position of returning to her marriage as though nothing had disturbed its security or of telling Torvald herself. Krogstad even offers to withdraw it, but Kristine, seeing the importance of honesty in the Helmers' marriage, will not hear of the idea. In each of these critical moments, Ibsen presents his audience with a dramatic question: What will happen now that Krogstad is not home to receive Kristine? What will Nora do now that Torvald will read the letter? Will Torvald do the "wonderful thing," that is, accept the blame and the responsibility, as Nora wishes he will?

The play is a deftly constructed series of such questions that are answered by subsequent scenes, which themselves raise new questions. But unlike *Oedipus*, *A Doll House* does not create an inexorable movement to the end. At any point, we feel, justifiably, that disaster might be avoided. What is important is that given the way in which each dramatic question is resolved, the particular ending Ibsen chose is not inconsistent with earlier action. An older generation may be offended morally by Nora's choice, but they must agree that given all they have seen of Nora's character and the progression of the plot, the ending, though not the only possible one, is dramatically right.

Having invaded the dollhouse through the front door, the back door, and the chimney, I feel as though I am in, and the students are there with me. Not only have the students done a thorough job of analyzing the play itself, so also have they been initiated into drama through a play that can serve as a model for the creation of character and dramatic action. Through controlled discussion, which, depending on the loquaciousness of the group, can take anywhere from three to six fifty-minute sessions, the students have dissected the corpse of this 1879 play and found it decidedly alive.

Ibsen and the Well-Made Play

Cary M. Mazer

A plan is to a play what it is to a house: the first condition of its beauty and stability. You may overload a building with the most magnificent decoration, you may use the most solid materials: if it is not erected in accordance with the laws of equilibrium and due proportion, that building will neither please nor last. The same holds good of a dramatic story. It must first of all be clear; and without a plan there can be no clarity. It must proceed without a stop to a defined goal; without a plan such a progression is impossible. The dramatic story must assign to each character his proper position; each action must be placed at a precise point; without a plan, there can be no regard to proportion. The plan includes not only the *order* of events, but also what Alexandre Dumas the elder called the first article of the playwright's creed, the art of preparing situations; in other words, of logically and naturally leading up to them.   (Matthews 265)

Thus wrote Ernest Legouvé, the French nineteenth-century playwright, about the lessons of dramatic art he learned from his collaborator and mentor, Eugène Scribe, the prolific dramatist and librettist who, in the 1830s, created a new model of dramatic structure, the *pièce bien-faite*, or well-made play. It is clear from this passage that the success of the well-made play was based on the playwright's ability to tell a dramatic story while generating the maximum interest and excitement in the audience. Following Aristotle, the well-made play emphasized action, or plot, over character; but it carried this emphasis well beyond what Aristotle could have imagined, developing a set of prescriptions and formulas for the creation of dramatic tension that provided the model for virtually every successful dramatist for the rest of the century.

Did Ibsen write well-made plays? This has been the subject of some debate over the years. As the dramaturge for the Norwegian Theater in Bergen from 1851 to 1857, Ibsen had a hand in the production of many Continental plays by Scribe and his followers, and the case has been made (using Ibsen's early *Lady Inger of Østraat* as an example) that he certainly knew the mechanics of the genre. Michael Meyer, among others, identifies non-Scribean models for this play and denies any debt to the genre (Meyer, *Biography* 297). While no literary detective work can prove or disprove Ibsen's debt to Scribe (whose work Ibsen called "dramatic candy floss" [Meyer, *Biography* 71]), Ibsen's technical affinities with the well-made play are inescapable, not just in the early verse plays but in the prose social plays in particular. Ibsen may have been more interested in character than in plot, in the psychological histories and experiences of his characters as they react to the problems of contemporary society and the agonies of their spiritual states; and he made significant advances in the means that the dramatist can employ to present and to reveal the workings of character and the pressures of society. But he was nonetheless a dramatic storyteller, conceiving dramatic situations, letting his stories unfold, according to patterns, if not rules, that his audience could understand and that would sustain their interest. The well-made play was not just a formula; it was a way of thinking about the drama that permeated the artistic sensibilities of the nineteenth-century theatrical community. Our question ought not to be Did Ibsen write well-made plays? but What can the well-made play tell us—and our students—about the way Ibsen viewed the drama and about the way he structured the theatrical experiences of his audience? Understanding the mechanics of the genre can help us understand Ibsen's craft as a dramatist, can enable us, in fact, to distinguish between the talents of Ibsen the craftsman and the genius of Ibsen the dramatic artist.

It is fairly easy to acquire a working understanding of the major features of the well-made play. The goal of the well-made play is the stimulation of the audience's interest, and the principal medium is the plot. Legouvé compared a play to an express train (Matthews 88); Bernard Shaw's metaphor for the well-made play is the mechanical rabbit used in dog racing (*Our Theatres* 2: 14). In either case, the plot is a carefully tooled and fully wound mechanism, carrying the audience forward through the play via intrigues, confrontations, and complications.

The well-made play usually has a late "point of attack," beginning the story near the moment of greatest action and conflict and employing an early, somewhat lengthy exposition to establish the salient background facts. Facts are important commodities, for the audience and, moreover, for the character. Dramatic energy in the well-made play derives principally from the struggle of characters for power over one another, and that power is often based on information: what one person knows of the other's secrets can be used to advantage. Big dramatic scenes often involve the public disclosure of hitherto secret information. The audience is occasionally left in the dark about critical information until key moments in the drama. But, just as often, the audience knows more than the characters do. This frequently leads to a standard feature of the well-made play, the *qui pro quo*, a scene in which each character is party to different essential information and both are mistaken in the belief that they are talking about the same subject; in other words, each character takes "this for that" in decoding the signals of the other. The *qui pro quo* invariably complicates the plot and adds to the audience's delight and sense of tension. A classic *qui pro quo* from English comedy appears in *The Importance of Being Earnest*, when Gwendolyn and Cecily quarrel after they both boast of their engagement to Ernest Worthing; each has a different man in mind who she thinks is named Ernest, and neither knows that no one by that name actually exists.

Since facts are so crucial to the action of the well-made play, they often take the form of letters, telegrams, secret messages, objects, or signals charged with special meaning for the characters party to the vital information. Tension is built over the issue of who will have access to the letter or object, when it will be found, whether it will be intercepted or misinterpreted, and so forth.

The *scène à faire* is the moment of critical confrontation between opposing forces and often the scene in which the information previously hidden from the audience is revealed. William Archer, Ibsen's English translator and an unshakeable advocate of the importance of dramatic construction, translates *scène à faire* as "the obligatory scene," the event that the logic of the plot has made inevitable and that the audience has been led to expect. It is the destination toward which the entire design of the play has been pointing; Legouvé confesses quite frankly that a well-made play is written "by beginning at the end," that is, by devising the *scène à faire* and then writing the play that prepares for it (Matthews 87). The well-made play then ends with a *dénouement,*where all the mysteries are solved and the knots unraveled as the several strands of the plot are neatly tied up.

I usually ask my students, in both undergraduate modern drama survey courses and graduate courses, to read at least one well-made play before reading Ibsen and to diagram its construction and devices. Analyzing plays of negligible literary value, with shallow characters and simplistic theses, encourages the student to distinguish between structure and content, between the technical and the artistic. The student also learns to recognize the structural features of the well-made play in other, more sophisticated pieces. Readers are often so entranced by Ibsen's dramatic situations and so fascinated by his characters that they fail to distinguish between what they know about a character and how they came to know it, between what happens in the drama and how the dramatist chose to let the events unfold. The thrill of reading *A Doll House* results from the same features that make the play exciting in the theater: the dramatist "prepares his situations" and "assigns each character his proper position" according to the "plan" of the play, as Legouvé would put it, according to the resources at his disposal. And while Ibsen's didactic goals, his deep understanding of his characters, and, particularly in the later plays, the symbolic resonances of the drama are quite beyond the priorities of the well-made play, he reflexively drew from its formulas for his palette of theatrical effects.

The student can quickly recognize many of the features of the well-made play that find their way into the plan of *A Doll House*. Ibsen employs a late point of attack and uses Nora's reunion with Mrs. Linde after ten years to provide the necessary exposition: one need only compare the structure of *A Doll House* with Shaw's summary of the plot in *The Quintessence of Ibsenism* or with the opening sequences of the Jane Fonda film version to appreciate how late Ibsen's point of attack really is. With Mrs. Linde, we become party to the "little secrets" that Nora has kept from Torvald: her secret debt, her means of saving and repayment, and her reason for taking Torvald on the southern vacation. We learn, before Mrs. Linde does, the identity of her secret creditor. And we learn, with Nora, about the power that Krogstad holds in his knowledge of her forgery, a concrete document that Nora must keep from her husband. The main "action" of the play hinges on the timing of the delivery of Krogstad's letter and on the moment when Torvald reads its contents. The arrival of the letter in the mail slot, Nora's attempt to pick the lock, and Torvald's promise to read the mail after the party all contribute to the rising dramatic tension.

Ibsen employs several *qui pro quo* sequences. At the end of act 1, Torvald is asked about the gravity of Krogstad's crime, and his answer inadvertently convinces Nora of her unsuitability as a mother. In act 2, Mrs. Linde wrongly guesses the identity of Nora's creditor and in doing so gives Nora the idea of asking Dr. Rank for money. In perhaps the most puzzling and provocative scene in the play, Nora flirts with Dr. Rank in order to ask him for monetary help and instead elicits an unwelcome confession of love. And one need stretch the definition only a little to include that embarrassing sequence in the final act when Torvald tries to seduce Nora after they return from the party.

There are, of course, significant departures from the structure of the well-made play in *A Doll House*. Given the lengths to which Ibsen has gone to establish what is essentially a blackmail plot, centering on the disclosure of a past crime and the effect it will have on Krogstad's power over Nora and over Torvald, the playwright's departure from the expected complication and denouement generate some of the play's most stunning and, I believe, most precisely calculated dramatic effects. One such departure is Mrs. Linde's decision to let Torvald read Krogstad's letter even after Krogstad has offered to withdraw it; she deliberately precipitates the crisis that Nora has been trying all along to avoid. The other departure is deliberate thwarting, not so much of our expectations as of Nora's. Critics inclining toward meta-dramatic interpretations might view Nora's anticipation of the "miracle" as a scenario of dramatic events, of a particular denouement that, she expects, will follow from the disclosure of information in the *scène à faire*. Nora's misplaced faith is, of course, one of the central themes of the play, an inability to distinguish between the "two kinds of spiritual law" and the "two kinds of conscience" that characterize men and women (Ibsen, *Workshop* 91). Torvald's reactions to the blackmail note and to Krogstad's second, vindicating letter are so different from what Nora expected that the play's well-made machinery grinds to a halt and, simultaneously, Nora's faith in the world, as she understood it, shatters.

The denouement that follows is not what the well-made structure of the play led us to anticipate. Shaw thought that the final discussion between Nora and Torvald was the "technical novelty" of Ibsen's dramaturgy: "Formerly you had in what was called a well made play an exposition in the first act, a situation in the second, and unravelling in the third. Now you have exposition, situation, and discussion; and the discussion is the test of the playwright" (*Quintessence* 171). But it is not Ibsen's use of the discussion per se that makes this scene so technically innovative; rather, it is the way Ibsen precisely controlled audience interest and expectations by deliberately manipulating the formulas of the contemporary drama. Such reconstructions enabled him to transcend the mechanical patness of the well-made play's denouement and to carry his character to a higher level of self-discovery and awareness.

By analyzing *A Doll House* in the light of the techniques and devices of the well-made play, the student can become sensitized to the craftsmanship involved in the process of dramatic storytelling in the nineteenth century and begin to share in Ibsen's own creative process. While it may not be possible to retrace this process with total certainty, the notes, scenarios, and drafts for *A Doll House* anthologized in *From Ibsen's Workshop* can give the student some idea of Ibsen's conscious crafting of his dramatic material. Most of the changes from the penultimate draft to the final version involve details that contribute to our understanding of the characters, but several changes are structural. All the scenes that are recognizable as *qui pro quos,* for example, were added only in the final draft. Indeed, an entire discussion of Krogstad's crime in the middle of the first act has been cut from the earlier version so that the information can be revealed by Torvald in the dialogue at the end of the first act. Ibsen, it would seem, had invented his characters and the basic situation of the play; only in the final version did he strengthen his dramatic storytelling by drawing more explicitly upon the standard devices of the well-made play.

The nature of the dramaturgical process can be made even more immediate for students through exercises that enable them to experience firsthand the act of telling a story in dramatic form. One cannot expect students to be able playwrights, but they can learn *numérotage*, the planning of the sequence of scenes. One exercise that has proved rather successful is to ask students to take a well-made play they have read and to create a new scenario for it as though it were written by Ibsen or, conversely, to take an Ibsen play and to redraft it as though it were written by Scribe. They should try to get beyond the relatively superficial differences of style and depth of characterization and to concentrate on structural aspects. They will discover, of course, that many of the basic narrative strategies will remain unchanged; major departures will occur instead in the nature of the crisis that the mechanism of the plot generates and in the effects that the crisis may have on the development of the characters and their awareness of the social and interpersonal worlds around them.

Another exercise is to have the students construct afresh a scenario for one of Ibsen's plays. For example, the teacher could easily use Ibsen's initial notebook entry for *A Doll House*, in tandem with the story of Laura Kieler, which Ibsen used as a model for his drama. The student would then sketch out the basic motivations of the characters, list the information that each character knows at any given time, invent situations that would generate the necessary intrigue, and write out a scenario for how these situations would be established and developed. If the students are well versed in the structural features of the well-made play, they will have a broad repertoire of effects from which to draw, and they will be particularly challenged by the task of finding a set of situations that will successfully dramatize Ibsen's chosen theme. If *A Doll House* has become too familiar, the teacher can use other plays by Ibsen or an assortment of other preparatory material. Possible alternatives include Ibsen's discarded description of the major characters in *The White Horses*, which he drastically revised for *Rosmersholm*, or his first notebook entry for *Hedda Gabler*. The teacher can prepare a narrative sketch for the theme and situation of, say, *Ghosts* or *The Wild Duck* and ask students to give these situations dramatic form before reading Ibsen's versions. Or students could take Shaw's narrative renderings of the plays and prepare more detailed dramatic scenarios.

The specific skills that all these exercises are designed to generate are no substitute for the actual interpretation of the plays themselves. But they are essential in any course that approaches drama generally or traces the development of dramaturgy over a period. And I suspect that an awareness of the dramaturgical devices of the well-made play would be of considerable value, even when the instructional emphasis is on theme, character, or language. Once my students feel at home with the plays of Ibsen, they move on to Strindberg, Wedekind, Maeterlinck, and Chekhov. They find that they can no longer understand the characters, their biographies, or their motivations as they could for Ibsen: the dramatic events are no longer as logical or coherent, and the evidence on which students base their interpretations is not as readily at hand. It is only then that they can look back to Ibsen and appreciate not only what they know, say, about Nora's character but how and why Ibsen chose to let them know it. They can see the system of logic and causality, the pattern of dramatic action, the structuring of events that were all-important parts of Ibsen's understanding of the dramatic medium. And they can consequently begin to decode the system of dramatic signification that Ibsen's successors employed, and so begin a new process of interpretation. For it is only through an understanding of the playwright's control of the theatrical medium and an appreciation of the audience's experience of the play in performance that the reader can approach a play on its own terms. The detection of the well-made dramaturgy of A *Doll House* is only one stage in the process of acquiring this appreciation.

A Marxist Approach to *A Doll House*

Barry Witham and John Lutterbie

Theatrical production is a process that illuminates the dramatic text, and criticism is the tool that enables theater artists to make the most effective choices. This is the central premise of Drama 102 (Play Analysis), in which we discuss eight or so plays from a variety of critical viewpoints. Although some of the plays lend themselves more readily to a particular kind of analysis (such as a Jungian reading of *The Emperor Jones*), we point out that this affinity should not exclude additional insights that can be gained from a structuralist or feminist reading. We stress that criticism is a preamble to production and that plays are complex and multifaceted. Moreover, we discourage the theatrical sleight of hand that frequently reduces plays to a single metaphor, and we encourage our students to view drama through the lenses of differing approaches.

In teaching *A Doll House* we first examine the text from a traditional point of view stressing historical and biographical considerations. We review Ibsen's commitment to women's rights and his interest in the career of Laura Kieler, who some critics believe was the model for Nora. Indeed, F. L. Lucas has stated that "one cannot fully understand Nora without knowing something of the strange, yet true story of Laura Kieler" (131). By comparing the two women it is possible to watch Ibsen's heroine emerge from the despair and pain that characterized much of Kieler's life.

Still, the historical and biographical approach is limiting, and our next step is to explore the play through another lens. (The metaphor of the "lens" we have found to be particularly effective since it implies that there are no right or wrong interpretations but rather discoveries that can be made by studying a play from more than one vantage point.) The critical method that has stimulated many of our recent students—and that concerns us here—is a Marxist reading of the play. Marxist criticism is a complex topic, and, as the recent work of Fredric Jameson, Henri Arvon, and Raymond Williams exemplifies, critical methodologies vary widely. Moreover, many American students come to Marxist aesthetics with reluctance, conditioned partly by a distrust of all things Russian. Thus we try to emphasize specific issues on which critics agree, and we assign short readings from Terry Eagleton's *Marxism and Literary Criticism* as a point of departure.

It is important, of course, to review Marx's early writings with their humanistic focus and analysis of class structure. Notions of the dialectic and of human alienation are productive ways of introducing students to Marx since alienation seems to be a concept with which they can identify. This approach has the added value of breaking down some initial prejudices toward the subject matter. By stressing the human side of Marx's work, we can reduce student resistance and encourage a more objective view of the social analysis that follows.

We then talk about the text of the play as an objectification of the author's idea, a process that is a creative act but that in dialectical terms is imperfect because it can never completely express Ibsen's vision or totally repress unconscious ideas that shape the text. Drawing on both Terry Eagleton and Louis Althusser (*Lenin and Philosophy*), we define ideology as a false consciousness, a system of beliefs and ideas that functions to disguise the inequities of a class-based society. Using this definition to examine the play, we stress the concept that ideology is shaped by both what is in the text (Torvald's domination of Nora) and by what is "absent" (Nora's relationship with her mother). One of the primary goals of any Marxist analysis is the investigation of ideological content, and the existence of this content allows Marxist critics to argue that all works of art are political. This is a highly controversial point with many students, and the discussions often become heated as we examine its implications.

We then focus on the economic realities of Ibsen's world. *A Doll House* is especially suited to this type of examination because the bank—an obvious and blatant symbol for money—stands at the center of the play. Torvald has just been appointed manager. Mrs. Linde wants to work there, as does Krogstad. And Nora's jubilance at the beginning of the play is directly related to the financial security ensured by Torvald's new job. Moreover, an economic analysis quickly reveals how the consciousness of the characters is shaped and determined by their class and status. Even though Downs has argued that "except for three virtual supernumeraries, all the persons of the play belong to the educated middle class" (*Study* 111), it is clear that class differences do exist. Torvald stands for the moneyed elite—in this case the bank owners—while Mrs. Linde and Krogstad function as workers struggling to maintain a subsistence income.

A principal tenet of Marxist criticism is that human consciousness is a product of social conditions and that human relationships are often subverted by and through economic considerations. Mrs. Linde has sacrificed a genuine love to provide for her brothers, and Krogstad has committed a crime to support his children. Anne-Marie, the maid, has also been the victim of her economic background. Because she's "a girl who's poor and gotten in trouble" (Fjelde, *Complete Plays* 155), her relationship with her child has been interrupted and virtually destroyed. In each instance the need for money is linked with the ability to exist. But while the characters accept the social realities of their misfortunes, they do not appear to question how their human attitudes have been thoroughly shaped by socioeconomic considerations.

Once students begin to perceive how consciousness is affected by economics, a Marxist reading of Ibsen's play can illuminate a number of areas. Krogstad, for example, becomes less of a traditional villain when we realize that he is fighting for his job at the bank "as if it were life itself" (145). And his realization of the senselessness of their lives is poignantly revealed when he reflects on Mrs. Linde's past, "all this simply for money" (177). Even Dr. Rank speaks about his failing health and imminent death in entirely financial terms. "These past few days I've been auditing my internal accounts. Bankrupt! Within a month I'll probably be laid out and rotting in the church-yard" (162).

All these characters, however, serve as foils for the central struggle between Nora and Torvald and highlight the pilgrimage that Nora makes in the play. At the outset two things are clear: (1) Nora is enslaved by Torvald in economic terms, and (2) she equates personal freedom with the acquisition of wealth. The play begins joyfully not only because it is the holiday season but also because Torvald's promotion to bank manager will ensure "a safe, secure job with a comfortable salary" (129). Nora is happy because she sees the future in wholly economic terms. "Won't it be lovely to have stacks of money and not a care in the world?" (131).

What she learns, however, is that financial enslavement is symptomatic of other forms of enslavement—master-slave, male-female, sexual objectification, all of which characterize her relationship with Torvald—and that money is no guarantee of happiness. At the end of the play she renounces not only her marital vows but also her financial dependence because she has discovered that personal and human freedom are not measured in economic terms.

This discovery also prompts her to reexamine the society of which she is a part and leads us into a consideration of the ideology in the play. In what sense has Nora committed a criminal offense in forging her father's name? Is it indeed just that she should be punished for an altruistic act, one that cost her dearly both in terms of self-denial and the destruction of her family? Ibsen's defense of Nora is clear, of course, and his implicit indictment of a society that encourages this kind of injustice stimulates a discussion of the assumptions that created the law.

One of the striking things about *A Doll House* is how Anne-Marie accepts her alienation from her child as if it were natural, given the circumstances of class and money. It does not occur to her that laws were framed by other people and thus are capable of imperfection and susceptible to change. Nora broke a law that not only tries to stop thievery (the appropriation of capital) by outlawing forgery but also discriminates against anyone deemed a bad risk. Question leads to question as the class investigates why women were bad risks and why they had difficulty finding employment. It becomes obvious that the function of women in this society was not "natural" but artificial, a role created by their relationship to the family and by their subservience to men. In the marketplace they were a labor force expecting subsistence wages and providing an income to supplement that earned by their husbands or fathers.

An even clearer picture of Nora's society emerges when the Marxist critic examines those features or elements that are not in the play. These "absences" become valuable clues in understanding the ideology in the text. In the words of Fredric Jameson, absences are:

> terms or nodal points implicit in the ideological system which have, however, remained unrealized in surface of the text, which have failed to become manifest in the logic of the narrative, and which we can therefore read as what the text represses. (48)

The notion of absences is particularly intriguing for students, who learn quickly to apply it to such popular media as films and television (what can we learn about the experience of urban black Americans from sitcoms like *Julia* and *The Jeffersons*?). Absent from *A Doll House* is Nora's mother, an omission that ties her more firmly to a male-dominated world and the bank owners who promoted Torvald. These absences shape our view because they form a layer of reality that is repressed in the play. And an examination of this "repressed" material leads us to our final topic of discussion: What is the relation between this play and the society in which it was created and produced?

Most Marxist critics believe that there are only three possible answers: the play supports the status quo, argues for reforms in an essentially sound system, or advocates a radical restructuring. Though these options are seemingly reductive, discussion reveals the complexities of reaching any unanimous agreement, and students frequently disagree about Ibsen's intentions regarding reform or revolution. Nora's leaving is obviously a call for change, but many students are not sure whether this leave-taking is a way forward or a cul-de-sac for a system that is thoroughly controlled by the prevailing power structure. At this point we assign Robert Brustein's chapter on Ibsen in *The Theatre of Revolt* so that students can evaluate for themselves the extent to which Ibsen's stance was revolutionary and the extent to which *A Doll House* "torpedoed the ark" (37).

Viewing the play through the lens of Marxist aesthetics does make one thing clear. Nora's departure had ramifications for her society that went beyond the marriage bed. By studying the play within the context of its socioeconomic structure, we can see how the ideology in the text affects the characters and how they perpetuate the ideology. The conclusion of *A Doll House* was a challenge to the economic superstructures that had controlled and excluded the Noras of the world by manipulating their economic status and, by extension, their conscious estimation of themselves and their place in society.

Appendix

Course Outline of Drama 102: Play Analysis

Since this is a discussion course, active classroom participation is required. In addition to reading individual plays, students are required to read the appropriate chapters in *A Handbook of Critical Approaches to Literature* by Guerin, Labor, et al. For the sections on Marxism and feminism, further readings will be assigned by the instructor. Due dates for papers are indicated below.

Week 1
Introduction
The Precritical Response
Textual Criticism
Dramatic Structure
Death of a Salesman

Week 2
TRADITIONAL CRITICISM
Historical-Biographical
Moral-Philosophical
The Romans in Britain (Howard Brenton)
The Romans in Britain

Week 3
TRADITIONAL, cont.
Major Barbara
Major Barbara
Compare *Salesman*
Review

Week 4
FORMALISM
The New Critics
Kinds of Formalism
Virginia Woolf
Virginia Woolf

Week 5
FORMALISM, cont.
Oedipus
Oedipus
Compare *Major Barbara*
MIDTERM EXAMINATION

Week 6
MARXISM
MARXISM
A Doll House
A Doll House
    Paper number 1 due
A Doll House

Week 7
MARXISM, cont.
Death of a Salesman
Compare *Major Barbara*
FEMINISM
FEMINISM

Week 8
Uncommon Women (Wendy Wasserstein)
Uncommon Women
Compare *A Doll House*
FEMINISM, cont.
Compare *Major Barbara*

Week 9
PSYCHOLOGICAL-MYTH
PSYCHOLOGICAL-MYTH
Hamlet
Hamlet
Jung: *Emperor Jones*

Week 10
PSYCHOLOGICAL-MYTH, cont.
Dutchman (Amiri Baraka)
Compare *Oedipus*
Review
    Paper number 2 due

FEMINISM AND
A DOLL HOUSE

A Doll House in a Course on Women in Literature

Katharine M. Rogers

I teach *A Doll House* in Women in Literature, a middle-level course aimed at both majors and nonmajors. Our goal is to see how literature illuminates our understanding of the traditional roles of women in the family—daughter, sister, lover, wife, and mother. I choose works that stimulate discussion of fundamental issues such as the importance and attainability of equality in marriage and the nature and obligations of the mother-child relationship. We read the works in chronological order, noting attitudes and concerns typical of their time but looking particularly for themes that persist through all periods. For example, Sophocles's *Antigone* raises the same issue of conflicting masculine and feminine attitudes toward justice that Ibsen's *A Doll House* does. The theme of self-fulfillment versus duty to others carries over from Eliot's *The Mill on the Floss* to *A Doll House*, which comes right afterward; and we discuss similarities in attitudes of the male characters, such as Tom's assumption that Maggie should accept his opinions as sounder than hers and his resistance to her earning money independently. We go on from *A Doll House* to *Ghosts* or *Hedda Gabler* or both, each of which develops or complements themes raised in the earlier play. *Ghosts*, which shows a woman victimized by moral blackmail rather than by romantic illusion, demonstrates the baneful effects of pursuing duty to husband and son to the exclusion of duty to oneself. But Hedda, imprisoned like the other heroines in a stifling environment, destroys herself, as well as others, because she thinks only of her duty to herself.

In the context of a women's studies course, the critical opinion that Ibsen was not concerned specifically with women's freedom in *A Doll House* has no credibility. Nevertheless, at some point we consider his famous declaration, in his "Speech at the Banquet of the Norwegian League for Women's Rights" (1898), that he never "consciously worked for the women's rights movement" and was "not even quite clear as to just what this women's rights movement really is" (Sprinchorn, *Ibsen: Letters* 337). This statement can easily be explained by Ibsen's dislike for party affiliation, his objection to being reduced from an artist to a propagandist, and his belief that the important thing is human development rather than specific political rights. It is valuable to make this point in women's studies courses, which tend to become overpoliticized. Our students should also be reminded of the differences between their attitudes and those of the original audience of 1879, who would not have considered the Helmer marriage so obviously bad or Torvald's complacency self-evidently ludicrous. In fact, Ibsen was concerned lest the audience sympathize entirely with Torvald, and he therefore purposely overwrote Torvald's lines (Sprinchorn, "Ibsen and the Actors")—with the result that Torvald seems a caricature today and Nora's admiration for him seems fatuous. Similarly, we must not let contemporary enthusiasm for liberation lead us to oversimplify the ending into a happy triumph. Thinking of Nora's painful disillusionment, her parting from her children, and the uncertainties of her future independent career, Ibsen called his play "the tragedy of modern times." (See his preliminary notes, in McFarlane, *Oxford Ibsen* 5: 436.)

But most of our class time is spent exploring the major feminist issues raised in the play, first analyzing what Ibsen says about them and then evaluating his presentation in terms of our own experience. Looking beyond the differences in property laws and modes of speech between Ibsen's time and our own, we see how the economic dependency, patriarchal rationalizations, and chivalric illusions that Ibsen so brilliantly anatomized in the nineteenth-century Helmer marriage continue to influence men's and women's attitudes today.

Immediately in the opening dialogue, Torvald lectures Nora about squandering his money and doles out to her the amount he thinks proper; and Nora petitions and excuses her expenditures—just like the beggar she ultimately recognizes herself to be. Thus Ibsen shows us how economic dependence degrades women in a society where respect is based on earning power, where unpaid work in the home is not considered work. Ibsen goes on to show the exhilarating freedom, traditionally denied women, of having one's own money—when Nora asks for money as a Christmas present (and Torvald would rather give her anything else) or when she confides that she enjoyed the copying work she did at night because it made her feel like a man. Kristine, who was forced to marry to support her family, and Anne-

Marie, who was forced to give up her child to support herself, round out the picture of women's economic helplessness. Having explored what Ibsen said about economic oppression, we ask ourselves whether the conditions he exposed still prevail: To what extent do men still control money in the home and in society at large? Are women still thought to be doing nothing when they merely run their households? Are such women generally considered parasitic and extravagant? How many men are still more comfortable with dependent wives than with independent ones?

We then analyze the patriarchal rationalizations that govern Torvald's treatment of Nora—his assumption that logic and responsibility pertain to men, his belief that male honor is supremely important while female honor is too negligible to mention, his self-congratulation on the heroism with which he would defend her should the need arise. We note that he appreciates Nora's real or supposed deficiencies because he needs something to belittle her for. We proceed from there to the destructive interplay between Torvald and Nora—for of course he could not be what he is if she did not constantly feed his self-importance. When he orders her not to eat macaroons, she meekly agrees, then disobeys and lies to him like a naughty child (thus behaving in a way that would reinforce his feelings of superiority, if he should find out). When she wants something from him, she flatters and manipulates instead of asking directly, as an equal. She proves his charge that she does not understand the society she lives in when she declares her indifference to the well-being of anyone outside her family and defiantly asserts that the law would never prosecute the mother of three little children. Concealing her competence and strength, Nora makes every effort to appear the twittering lark Torvald believes and wants her to be.

Their relationship leads us to consider how couples reinforce each other's destructive behavior patterns and whether an oppressive or exploitative situation is possible without mutual connivance. We decide how much Nora's limitations are merely assumed by those who wish to patronize her (Torvald's assurance that she cannot deal with serious problems) and how much they are real (her blind confidence in her husband's strength and wisdom). To the extent that they are real, we look into their social causes—for example, limited education and experience confine one's sympathies; lack of authority encourages one to resort to lies and tricks to gain one's ends. We may contrast Nora with Kristine, a woman who has been forced to live in a hard world (and who also starts out patronizing Nora).

What my students find hardest to accept in Nora is her romantic illusion that Torvald will assume responsibility for her forgery; it strikes them as a ridiculously unwarranted expectation, as well as a humiliating admission of feminine weakness. We must recognize that Ibsen's deflation of romantic chivalry, which seems far-fetched and pointless now, was necessary in the nineteenth century, when chivalry was pervasively used to conceal the domination and exploitation of women. Having implied from the beginning the falsities of nineteenth-century patriarchal marriage, in which the husband protects his wife from life in return for her uncritical admiration and dependence, Ibsen clinches his point by subjecting masculine heroism to a test and showing that a woman cannot in fact trust it to protect her. Nora's longing for a romantic hero who will save her is not only demeaning; it cannot be fulfilled because it is false. Once required to sacrifice something to his grandiose ideals, Torvald dismisses love and heroics as irrelevant and chides Nora for her faith in them. Men teach women that love is all-important and pretend to believe it themselves, but they soon enough reveal their disbelief when put to the test. Nora, confined to private life, has simply taken at face value the myths she has been taught about romantic love. While the ideal of chivalry may no longer be sufficiently credited to be worth attacking, we can profitably discuss other aspects of idealized romantic love. What is the difference between loving and being in love with? Must traditional romantic expectations be changed if marriage is to become egalitarian?

Having accounted for Nora's romantic illusions about her breach of the law, we concentrate on those aspects of her behavior that persist in ourselves. This can be a useful exercise in self-knowledge. I confess that on seeing *A Doll House* for the first time I was actually filled with rage—it must have been because I saw too much of myself in Nora, being patronized and acquiescing in that patronage. We would like to believe that we have nothing in common with the little lark, but how many of us are altogether liberated from traditional sexual role-playing? How effectively do we deal with men's assumptions of superiority? Don't we, in fact, sometimes confirm those assumptions by acting cute or use them to flatter men into giving us what we want? Do we always react appropriately to belittlement if the tone is playful? Are we not occasionally tempted to forego equality for sexual tributes and chivalrous protectiveness, even though we are more aware than Nora of the diminution these imply?

Finally, our class discusses two general moral issues important to feminists. First, do we agree with Ibsen's opinion, stated in his preliminary notes and dramatized in the play, that women and men have completely different concepts of law and conscience? Or should we attribute it to sexual stereotyping, based on the fact that most of the women he knew were confined to private life? If there are differences, are they natural or acquired? Have the increased education and experience of women since Nora's day changed their concepts of justice? Men have defined justice in abstract and sociological terms, ignoring the values important to women and then finding women wanting. Should women disprove masculine sneers by proving they can understand abstract justice as clearly as men can? Or should they strive to realize a new standard where consideration for a sick husband or a dying father outweighs the letter of the law? Do women naturally respond more to the concrete, the personal, the familial? And if so, should they use this sensitivity to modify society's concept of justice?

Second, there is the even more fundamental issue of duty to oneself, an issue that becomes ever more acute as women become increasingly unwilling to sacrifice themselves to the family. If women put their self-realization first, as men have traditionally done, what will happen to dependent others? The conflict between Nora's duty to herself and her duty to her children (if not to Torvald) must not be minimized. Can women take care of their duty to their children by redividing responsibilities in the home? Is everyone's first duty, as Nora comes to feel, to think out his or her own values and face reality without illusions? Is this self-development, in fact, necessary for adequacy as a parent? Can a woman who is not a mature human being be a good mother? (In this connection I mention Ibsen's suggestion, in his notes for *A Doll House*, that many nineteenth-century mothers might well go away and die, like insects, once they had completed the work of physical propagation.) How can one reconcile necessary self-realization with fulfilling the obligations of conventional social roles? (Torvald, Nora says, must learn to live independently of her as she must of him.) How can one be independent in marriage? How is it that Kristine will apparently find fulfillment in the relationship that Nora must reject in order to find herself? What is the difference between the Helmer marriage (and Kristine's first one, where she "sold herself" for her dependent mother and brothers) and the one she will make with Krogstad, since there too she will be working for him and his children?

In short, I try to make my students see how Ibsen illuminates the way women and men still interact, raises questions that still need to be asked, and suggests answers that still apply. *A Doll House* continues to remind us that we are not as liberated as we would like to believe.

Appendix

Syllabus for Women in Literature
Sophocles, *Antigone*
Euripides, *Medea*
Shakespeare, *Antony and Cleopatra*
Austen, *Pride and Prejudice*
Eliot, *The Mill on the Floss*
Ibsen, *A Doll House* and *Hedda Gabler*
Strindberg, *The Father*
Shaw, *Mrs. Warren's Profession*
Woolf, *To the Lighthouse*
Chopin, *The Awakening*
Lurie, *The War between the Tates*

Nora's Uncertainty

Irving Deer

I teach *A Doll House* (using Rolf Fjelde's translation and title) in an upper-division undergraduate course in modern drama. The class, generally about twenty students, is almost evenly split between majors and nonmajors. Since *A Doll House* is the first play of about a dozen assigned, it serves to introduce some of the main concepts to be developed in the course. I particularly stress the growing sense of the inadequacy of received traditions and conventions, both social and artistic. By focusing on this concept, I not only can get at the complexity of the play but also can relate *A Doll House* to the work of Strindberg, Chekhov, and Shaw, the other writers in the first half of the course.

There is not enough space here to make comparisons, except to say that Strindberg's *Miss Julie*, Chekhov's *Cherry Orchard*, and Shaw's *Heartbreak House* all show the dissolution of traditions. Thus a valuable way to approach *A Doll House* is to consider how it deals with decaying values and conventions. Nora's final discussion with Torvald shows that she is leaving him to learn for herself ("to educate herself") whether she is justified in finding the roles allowed her by tradition and convention—those of child, wife, and mother—inadequate. Despite her outright statements to that effect, however, most modern readers tend to see, though not always to like, the ending as an assertion of Nora's rights as an emancipated woman. According to Robert Brustein, for example, "Nora's abrupt conversion from a protected, almost infantile dependent into an articulate and determined spokesman for individual freedom" is a major flaw in the play (*Theatre* 49). Most students would agree with Raymond Williams that Ibsen intends everything, including the final slamming of the door, as an affirmation of Nora's right to personal freedom from the vain and repressive forces of society represented by her husband (48–49). But why, then, after Nora leaves, does Ibsen have Torvald express his misery and hope, his distress and confusion? If Torvald is the insensitive, vain, even grotesque character so many critics take him to be (e.g., see Gray 43), why does Ibsen show him in such pain, straining so to grasp what is happening?

Such counterevidence—and, as we shall see, there is a great deal more—is largely ignored by readers eager to embrace the melodramatic polemical conclusions about the play that our social reform climate of opinion has for at least two decades promoted. The Jane Fonda version of the play, for example, expresses such a view. After all, many students think, is not the play generally considered a "problem play"? What could the "problem" be but the rights of women or at least of individuals, women or men? What

could the play itself be but a skillful diatribe against the injustices of repressive traditions and conventions? Moreover, parts of the play support
such an interpretation. Nora says she is no longer in love with Torvald
because he didn't fulfill her romantic-heroic expectations when he saw Krogstad's letter. She had expected him to defy Krogstad, to take the blame on
himself, but instead, she says, he gave in to Krogstad's terms. These remarks
seem to justify a melodramatic view of the play two ways: first, by indicating
that Torvald is not the hero his long-suffering wife had hoped he would be
and, second, by indicating that he has given in to the character Ibsen has
made most like a melodramatic villain. We can easily imagine Krogstad
twirling his mustache as he waves his papers in front of the nose of the
heroine before tying her to the railroad tracks.

This fantasy is not too farfetched to our students because, as Raymond
Williams confirms, Ibsen seems to have framed the action in terms of melodramatic heroes and villains (50). When we first see Nora, she is hiding her
macaroons from Torvald. We soon learn that intrigues of every kind, trivial
and serious alike, are required of her in Torvald's world. She has continually
had to intrigue to get money to pay back Krogstad and to keep the loan a
secret from her husband. Later, in the central intrigue of the play, she
attempts to stop Torvald from getting the mail, establishing a kind of Scribean
intrigue ambience to the action. The melodramatic conventions of the well-
made play were, after all, the school in which Ibsen learned his craft.

Both Torvald and Krogstad are so much like stereotypical villains, and
Nora is so much like a stereotypical heroine, that we have difficulty seeing
them as anything else. Torvald is incredibly vain and oblivious to Nora's
torment. He imagines that her every thought is and ought to be devoted to
his every whim and desire. Even in her most desperate need, she cannot
discuss her problems with him because she knows, and we are shown, that
he will only make things worse. Because he is the one above all others who
should help her but will not, we accept Torvald as an arrogant melodramatic
fool. Add to that Krogstad's original determination to have his way even if
he ruins the life of a young mother of three, and we have what seems a
perfect pair of villains, both determined to destroy the innocent heroine.

After presenting the play to students in these terms, I begin to point out
evidence for the opposite, but still melodramatic, interpretation, one that
sees *Nora* as vain and self-centered, determined to have her way no matter
what the consequences. This was the view of most critics when the play first
came out, and it was established as a serious if not major critical tradition
by Hermann Weigand in *The Modern Ibsen* in 1925. Weigand disciples
today, like Richard F. Dietrich, are still energetically espousing his view,
as unpopular as it may seem.

The question I now raise with students is not what we think of Nora but what Ibsen seems to think of her. Is he praising or blaming her? That the play ends on the note of Torvald's despair seems to argue against Ibsen's intention to praise her for heroic determination. In addition, Ibsen often seems to be satirizing Nora. Even students who gloss over the ending can hardly deny how silly Nora appears as she eats her macaroons, plays squirrel, tells her little lies to Torvald, practices her little intrigues, flirts with Dr. Rank, childishly imagines committing suicide or being romantically saved by Torvald. Nora's confusion—even at the end she seems certain one minute, uncertain the next, about what is right or wrong—her manipulation of Torvald, her play-acting, the distress she causes Dr. Rank in her little flirtation— all these details and others may be meant to indicate that she is far from the perfect heroine. She also did, after all, commit the forgery Krogstad accuses her of, and she did so in the naive way he describes.

Once students recognize that the play contains evidence for contradictory melodramatic interpretations, I can ask why Ibsen might be including such evidence. Why does he seem both to praise and to blame Nora? Is he trying to show us the inadequacy and partiality of both ways of seeing the events? Either interpretation leaves out the other and leaves out too much that is obvious and important. Moreover, each is based on a melodramatic view of experience. Is Ibsen trying to show us not simply the inadequacy and partiality of either melodramatic interpretation but also the inadequacy of melodrama itself as a way of interpreting modern experience? The limitations of viewing the world from so simple a perspective seem to be more nearly Ibsen's point than praising or blaming Nora. Ibsen brings this lesson home to us by enticing us into one extreme, then the other.

Ibsen's shifting perspective helps us share the problematic sense of the world Nora and his other characters experience, their growing doubts about all the old accepted truths and about the traditions and conventions that sustained those truths. What certainty we may at first experience about the melodramatic world Ibsen seems to be presenting is suddenly undermined when we pass from the certainty of one melodramatic view of Nora to the uncertainty of two contradictory views. This experience reflects Nora's, as she goes from certainty to uncertainty, gradually questioning all her old convictions about love, about having a happy, secure marriage and fulfilling the duties of a wife and mother, about living a dignified life in a just society. Seeing the play this way allows us to recognize and experience its richness and complexity. The play is about that process, about the way in which Nora experiences the growing uncertainty of her time, not about any argument for or against her.

Just as Ibsen discourages the reader from seeing his characters as mere melodramatic stereotypes, Nora herself is trying to keep from being reduced. She wants to curse like a man, sign loans, have male friends, and enjoy some personal power, not because she wants to be a man but because she wants to express more of herself than society allows. When she tries to talk to Rank as a friend, he assumes she wants to be his lover, the only role open to Nora outside wife and mother. She must cut off her attempt to reach him as a friend.

Students can now understand another important idea: that a stereotyped view of the play, the characters, and the situations cuts off any further thought or feeling about the things stereotyped. Seeing as decisive the slamming of the door at the end of the play denies the openness implied in Nora's mentioning the possibility, however remote, that she and Torvald might get together again. Torvald's melodramatic rejection of Nora when he reads Krogstad's first letter closes off their relationship. In effect he dismisses her from the human race, since he denies her the only roles permitted her, those of wife and mother, thus ironically pushing her toward finding new ways to relate to society. When moments later he receives Krogstad's second letter and restores her to her status as delicate possession, she recognizes that he is once again trying to cut off her chance to grow and become involved with the world. She sees that he has put her back in a box. Students can see the inadequacy both of the social conventions Nora challenges and of the artistic conventions Ibsen was challenging.

What we see is that, followed rigidly and mechanically, conventions become means for manipulating and intimidating people, for preventing instead of facilitating communication. That is how conventions function for Torvald and most of the people in his society; that is why Nora cannot reach Torvald when she most needs his help and is forced to face her greatest crisis alone. She had believed that as child, wife, and mother, she was guaranteed security, dignity, and purpose. Now, suddenly, she discovers that Torvald, far from recognizing her sacrifice on his behalf, can and does deny her both status and dignity in order to preserve his own vanity. Everything she had thought certain is thrown into doubt. Conventions that seemed grounded in an absolute order of things now begin to seem arbitrary, based on power.

A Doll House is not limited to concern with Nora's changing vision; Ibsen shows how that vision is taking hold in society despite blindness and resistance. Nora may be the most conscious of the changes occurring in traditional values and conventions. But Torvald discovers at the end that, whether he can imagine it or not, Nora is leaving. The conventions he thought bound her to him—her duty to husband and children—simply are no longer working. Krogstad, too, thanks to Christine, sees the limitations of his role as melodramatic villain, the only way society has allowed him to act to save his children and his dignity. Even Rank discovers, albeit too late, that his hopes for a conventional lover relationship with Nora are futile.

But Nora remains the character who most exemplifies Ibsen's point. Understanding the reasons for her role-playing, intrigues, and erratic behavior is central to understanding the play. She pretends to be the obedient wife who does not eat macaroons or waste money, the supportive wife who does not criticize her husband, the loving and dedicated wife-dancer who follows her husband's every direction—all to cover up her growing sense that the roles Torvald and society keep demanding of her are destroying her because they require her to lie about some of the most important aspects of her life. When she can no longer cover up her most important unconventional acts— the forgery and the loan—she has to recognize that she cannot go on playing these stifling roles. Whether she will go on to follow traditional conventions in new, less stifling ways or discover conventions-to-be, she does not at this stage know. What she and Ibsen do know, and students can be guided to learn, is that the heroic and romantic social conventions of the past were fast becoming stereotypes. That Ibsen could nevertheless use their artistic counterparts—the conventions of melodrama—to show their dissolution and the emergence of a modern consciousness is a tribute to his artistic mastery.

LEARNING THROUGH PERFORMING

The Opening Moments of *A Doll's House*: For Performance and Analysis in Class

J. L. Styan

One's first thoughts about teaching *A Doll's House* are likely to resemble those of contemporary critics of Ibsen and Ibsenism. The play's powerful theme of individualism and the sanctity of marriage in Victorian society, its intimate perception of domestic life, and its apparent—and unwelcome—promotion of women's rights firmly establish Ibsen as a great social realist in any literature and drama curriculum. For social relevance, indeed, this play and *Ghosts* constitute the most momentous pair in the story of the modern theater. They contain all that is needed to fuel the genre debate about naturalism, "modern tragedy," and the new play of ideas; to illustrate how the flash fire of avant garde reformist drama raced through the independent theater societies of Paris, Berlin, and London; and to exemplify how Ibsenism and the Ibsenites became a cultural issue in Western Europe at the end of the nineteenth century.

Of course, there is much more to Ibsen's plays, as revivals in the 1970s and 1980s have demonstrated. Technically brilliant, *A Doll's House* was not recognized in its own time as a dramaturgical advance; on the contrary, many considered the play tedious and lacking in dramatic action. Today, teachers find it particularly good for discussing dramatic structure, richness of characterization, the use of minor parts for parallelism, and the development of a well-made plot. The play also shows Ibsen's new confidence as an ironic comedian—in the depictions of the intimate relationship between husband and wife and in such extraordinary theatrical devices as Nora's use of a pair of silk stockings for flirting with Dr. Rank. It demonstrates Ibsen's growing sense of a visual drama and of the possibilities for a naturalistic symbolism, as in such a detail as the use of the Christmas tree, defiantly decorated with candles in act 1 and left in act 2 "stripped and dishevelled, its candles burned to their sockets" (quotations are from Michael Meyer's translation in Ghosts *and Three Other Plays*). It offers a scene that brings together with remarkable control and force the elements of good theater, verbal and musical, visual and balletic: it is the scene of Nora's frenzied dancing of the tarantella in her Italian costume with the multicolored shawl (soon to be covered by a black one before it is replaced in act 3 by her everyday clothes), the tambourine beating faster and faster to match the tension and crisis in the action as Nora simultaneously tries to distract Helmer's attention and to express her own tumultuous feelings. Above all, the play presents a new kind of dialogue, one that calls for a subtlety of realistic, psychologically sensitive acting, exemplified in the English-speaking theater by the work of Janet Achurch as Nora after 1889.

These features of dramatic originality in *A Doll's House* suggest that there are many points of departure for the discussion of this play and many sample scenes to scrutinize. Yet in its depictions of the behavior and relationships of the principal characters, and in its wealth of hints about their life before the play began, the text is so full of detail touching what is unspoken, so rich with oblique statements and subtextual implications, that almost any page can be used as a test of how the new realism can build up a conviction of truth in the minds of the audience and stimulate interest. It is helpful, therefore, to use class time to show how students unused to the interpretation of a play, and possibly new to Ibsen, can appreciate his work as a playwright.

If, before and after discussion, students are encouraged to act out the lines, much of the detail invisible to the reader will also emerge unpredictably, and the profit resulting from the exercise in close reading will be compounded immeasurably. For example, the opening dialogue between Nora and Helmer spoken through the closed door of his study enables Nora to show two kinds of behavior, the two faces of the doll wife that are missed in reading. It is worth remarking that the playwright mentioned the importance of this device in his earliest notes for the opening scene, and a simple "performance analysis" of the moment on stage helps students properly interpret the first page or two of the text.

Ibsen's habit of revision shows how much care he took with stage directions and his increasingly subtle use of settings to convey necessary information.

Decor can make important suggestions about period and place, even mood and atmosphere, as well as establishing the social and economic class of the characters. The "comfortably and tastefully, but not expensively furnished room" that the directions call for propose a late Victorian, middle-class, thoroughly "normal" background for the action of the play. Further details reveal something of the Helmers' family atmosphere: the piano makes this an inviting living room; such items as the carpet, the sofa, the armchairs, and especially the rocking chair in front of the porcelain stove suggest fashionable comfort, a settled and orderly domain, perhaps even the presence of children. The "engravings on the wall," the "what-not with china and other bric-a-brac," and "a small bookcase with leather-bound books" hint at modest pretensions to culture and sophistication. There is to be nothing remarkable about what is seen, no occasion for surprise or alarm. A fire burns in the stove and, as everyone who comes in from the outside will remind us, it is winter. The Victorian audience recognized it all.

Other details of the set warn of the action to come. Adjoining the main room are two areas, two avenues for retreat or escape, two extensions for the mind: Helmer's study, his inner sanctum, through a door on one side of the back wall, and through a door on the other side the world outside. Otherwise, this heart of the house will remain before our eyes throughout the play. For the moment, when the curtain rises, the stage is empty and the play begins in silence. The audience is first to assimilate the little domestic world it sees.

The class might be asked to say briefly what an audience looks for when a play begins. Besides the physical attributes of the actors—the surface indications of speech and behavior, the color of voice and the speed of speaking, the kind of gesture and movement—besides the "facts" of the situation as they are shown or spoken, the exposition characteristic of an Ibsen play includes the memories of the past that grant the characters their humanity, their flesh and blood. The audience will increasingly look for what lies under the surface of the speech and behavior: hidden feelings, implied relationships, the shared mood and spirit of the moment on stage. The realistic style of A Doll's House makes these questions the straightforward and familiar ones we ask of a real-life situation, as if we had just walked into the room ourselves.

The silence is broken by the front-door bell. Perhaps we also hear the footsteps of Helen, the maidservant. Then Nora makes a joyful entrance, loaded with parcels, laughing and "humming contentedly," her tune a jolly one. We are to remember this happy beginning when she makes her final exit from the play in act 3. When the Porter is seen carrying a Christmas tree at her heels, the occasion is identified and the mood apparently accounted for: the holiday is chosen for the force of its irony in the action to come. Nora's noisily whispered line to the maid, "Hide that Christmas tree away, Helen. The children mustn't see it—," adds to the mood of suppressed excitement and opens the play on a high note. The fresh, expectant tree is held for a moment center stage and is briefly admired before Helen whisks it away. Later in the act it will be returned to the middle of the room, and in act 2 its appearance will mark Nora's progress toward a harsher reality.

Our perception of life in this house now turns on Nora, prettily dressed, full of smiles. We respond to her youth and high spirits immediately, even to the touch of childlike delight in her instruction "Hide that Christmas tree away. . . . The children mustn't see it. . . ." The playwright goes on to provide her with a carefully chosen sequence of things to say and do, small incidents to help his audience build her character and begin the slippery process of making a moral assessment of her behavior. A strong signal is transmitted by her first little exchange with the Porter who carries in her purchases. When he asks for "fifty" (*öre*) for his services, Nora evidently does not have the right change or else deliberately gives him more than he asks for: she proffers a crown piece on the line, "Here you are. No—keep the change." Performance makes the point: does she give the man the larger coin with a careless air, thus declaring her indifference to money, or does she hesitate for just a moment before she says, "keep the change"? If the latter, we do not know for sure whether she is an irresponsible spendthrift or whether she considers that the spirit of the season calls for a gesture of generosity. From what we learn later of her effort to pay her debts from her housekeeping money, we should elect for the touch of ambiguity conveyed by her hesitation. The unanswered question lingers as we look for further clues to the mystery.

Nora next takes off her outdoor clothes, laughs again, and "takes from her pocket a bag of macaroons and eats a couple." In the opening scene this bag of macaroons is her personal prop, almost an extension of her personality, completing our image of her childlike qualities. A student actress can be used to demonstrate how the gesture is to be managed: a sly opening of the bag, perhaps a little laugh of pleasure, and a quick glance about her as she pops a macaroon into her mouth. When she "tiptoes" across the stage and listens at Helmer's study door, her behavior may now be more fully explained: she is acting as if a scolding parent may catch her in a guilty deed.

Yet there is an intriguing doubt. When she says to herself, "Yes, he's here," it is an unlikely line for a realistic play, unless she is also playing a role that she knows herself is unreal and somewhat theatrical. The movement of tiptoeing, unseen by anyone else on the stage at the time, together with the perplexing line itself, introduces a puzzling ingredient that perpetuates the element of ambiguity and that has to do with Nora's relationship with the unseen character, her husband. The ensuing dialogue through the closed door brilliantly enables us to perceive two Noras, the one she plays for Helmer and the other as herself. This further sign of ambiguity is confirmed when she "starts humming again" after she learns that her husband is in his room. It seems that she is now ready for him to see and hear her as she wishes to be seen and heard.

> HELMER (*from his room*).   Is that my skylark twittering out there?
> NORA (*opening some of the parcels*).   It is!
> HELMER.   Is that my squirrel rustling?
> NORA.   Yes!
> HELMER.   When did my squirrel come home?
> NORA.   Just now. (*Pops the bag of macaroons in her pocket and wipes her mouth.*) Come out here, Torvald, and see what I've bought.

From behind the door the childish endearments of "skylark" and "squirrel" seem to be invited, and the actress's singsong inflection in her "It is!" and "Yes!" should alert us to the game the wife is playing with her husband. How much of a game, how earnest a game, can only satisfactorily be revealed in performance. Then if she delays putting the bag of macaroons back into her pocket and wiping her mouth until the very last moment, it must be with the intention of having him spot her behaving like a child.

Helmer looks round his door after a calculated pause. He will do this as if it has become quite a habit for the two of them to greet each other like cat and mouse: the audience will measure his conduct by his wife's intimacy and familiarity with him when she runs to embrace him. This time his pen is still in his hand, however, as if he has truly been interrupted at his writing desk: "Bought, did you say?" The new note in his voice underscores the emerging motif of financial pressure. The skylark twittering and the squirrel rustling have become (in Meyer's translation) a "squanderbird . . . over-spending." The unreal language of diminutive animal life may not long survive the reality of being in debt. Is this relationship that of the cliché of the featherbrained wife who must be protected by a man who seems to be more of a father than a husband? Has Helmer's game with his child-bride sunk to the sentimental level of David Copperfield's relationship with his poor little Dora of, in Maurice Valency's words, a "scatterbrain" with a "pompous" husband (151)?

It would be easy to make this erroneous assumption. Helmer's apprehension and frown, his ready use of the term "squander," and his emphasis on the word "again" imply a familiar pattern, and Nora encourages what he is thinking. She displays the parcels artlessly. She finds a reason or two for spending the money: "Oh, Torvald, surely we can let ourselves go a little this year! . . . You're going to make lots and lots of money." Her words irritate him, and as he turns away in faint annoyance each time, she will chase after him, even to the point of trying to use her physical attraction to persuade him to her view:

HELMER. Well, you know. . . .
NORA. Oh yes, Torvald, we can. . . . Can't we? . . .
HELMER. Next year, yes. But. . . .
NORA. Pooh. . . .

This exchange, in the playing, can charm Helmer in his simplicity and enchant an audience. There need be no animosity, for the two are merely having a harmless domestic tiff, true to our picture of a nineteenth-century marriage in which the male is dominant without being in any way a tyrant. Essentially in this clever opening to *A Doll's House* the audience is to see a happy family and a normal home.

And yet surely an audience has good reason to hesitate before passing judgment on what it has just seen. Have we really watched a child enjoying the spirit of Christmas and taking a scolding from a wiser parent? Or have we been as deceived as Helmer himself by Nora's seeming ingenuousness?

An incongruity between what was on the surface and what beneath was present from the beginning, at least from the moment when the dialogue through the closed door began. Student players can rehearse and explore the telltale signs in the light of their knowledge that Nora has been anything but a spendthrift, that she is playing altogether another role with her husband. Indeed, another order of acting is required of the actress. The girl who opens her parcels with glee, the little bird who sings out to the authority figure behind the door, the naughty child who hides her forbidden macaroons and surreptitiously wipes her mouth, the charmer who slips her arms around her lover's neck and cajoles him with excuses—all are belied by the startling perception that Nora *prepared herself* for Helmer's appearance, even with a degree of cunning.

She displayed her parcels rather noisily, instead of concealing them. Her features were composed, even a little worried, as she responded (mechanically?) like a skylark and a squirrel. The naughty child must have known that her mouthful of macaroons (two at once, no less!) would be detected, as indeed it was: Helmer accuses her later of taking "a tiny little digression into a pastry shop." The coquetry was too well contrived, and the confidence of the coquette must have arisen from her previous successes in this line. She will of course behave naturally, with no obvious duplicity, for she is doing what comes easily to her as a young wife, behaving just as she did, perhaps, when she was a favorite daughter. She is no hypocrite. Nevertheless, later in the act she will say, with a surprising knowingness, "If only you knew how many expenses we larks and squirrels have." That, surely, is a breathtaking line.

The customary verdicts on this play, in both its time and our own, mostly focus on its theme. For some, the play represents a battle of the sexes that is "morbid and unwholesome," and "unnatural and immoral"; for others it is a manifesto for women's rights or a giant leap forward for the new reformist theater for others. All these points of view are valid. But the kind of exercise outlined in this performance approach to the text can also demonstrate the skill of the playwright, the accomplished way he engages his audience in the proper business of the theater. He does it the way it has been done by good dramatists over the centuries—by drawing us into the activity of building the play ourselves.

Performance as Criticism: *A Doll House* Scene Work in the English Classroom

Gay Gibson Cima

> The purpose of dramatic analysis is not to arrive at definitive inter-
> pretations of a work, but to discover and test dramatic possibilities.
> (Beckerman 405)

Ibsen's *A Doll House* is not a play. It is a script, a pretext for an action
to be discovered and completed by a director, actors, designers, and tech-
nicians; the play exists in performance. *A Doll House* thus carries within it
several possibilities for completion, each production an act of criticism, a
revelation of the director's conception of the script. Students who can en-
vision many productions of *A Doll House* and who can then select the subtlest
and richest as their own will be able to think and write more intelligently
about Ibsen's script and about drama in general.

This premise revolutionizes my undergraduate Ibsen-Strindberg class's
notions about dramatic literature. Accustomed to reading Shakespeare and
an occasional modern play script as poetic constructions, they both delight
in and fear the idea that they themselves must "complete" scenes from *A
Doll House*, whether in their minds or on the stage. To convince skeptics
of the necessity for this approach, I compare a dramatic script to a dance or
music score, reminding the English majors that although a novel is meant
to be read, a play script is designed for performance. Because students often
fail to understand the nature of the performance choices they face, as well
as the precision with which they should test those choices, I require that
they direct and enact scenes from the script. In their scene presentations
the student directors and actors cannot avoid selecting a critical viewpoint
or seeing the result of their failure to do so. Their fellow classmates, who
act as audience members and as critics, demand that each scene production
is justifiable in terms of the text and consistent within itself. I encourage
students to test a number of possible approaches to *A Doll House*, including
a metatheatrical approach emphasizing the self-dramatizing qualities of Nora
and Torvald.

Based on the early twentieth-century Russian director Constantin Stanislavski's blueprint for actors studying a script, this teaching methodology
places the fledgling director in a central role. The director must first determine the central action or "superobjective" of the script by discerning patterns, the shared character motivations that give the play its unique forward
motion. Stanislavski defines the "superobjective" of a script as its "inner
essence, the all-embracing goal, the objective of all objectives. . . . In Shake-

speare's tragedy of *Hamlet* such a superobjective would be the compre-
hending of the secrets of being. With Chekhov's *The Three Sisters* it is the
aspiration for a better life" (*Creating a Role* 78). (For a discussion of the
Aristotelian basis for this idea of action or superobjective, see Fergusson's
The Idea of a Theatre.) After the cast discusses the various superobjectives
that might encompass *A Doll House*, the director selects the "richest" approach, then blocks the scene and designs the set, costumes, and lights.
The actors formulate their "spines," or primary intentions throughout the
play, and their "beats," or moment-to-moment motivations, in keeping with
the director's vision. I ask them to be especially sensitive to the ways in
which they create each other's characters on stage: an excessively submissive
Nora dictates a bullying Torvald, for example, just as a manipulative Kristine
weakens Krogstad.

Two weeks before the class as a whole discusses *A Doll House*, I assign
scenes, designating directors and double casting when possible, so that the
students may weigh the relative merits of two completions of the same scene.
Five scenes (one per class, plus one meeting for a preliminary or a final
discussion) provide the focus of our *A Doll House* unit. The selected scenes
reveal the metatheatrical tendencies of the characters: (1) the act 1 opening,
(2) the act 2 tarantella, (3) Kristine and Krogstad's act 3 reconciliation, (4)
Rank's farewell and Torvald's discovery of Krogstad's letter in act 3, and (5)
the final encounter between Nora and Torvald. From the time the scenes
are assigned until two weeks later, when they are mounted in class, the
students read and reread *A Doll House*, discussing and then rehearsing their
scenes in the required minimum of four two-hour rehearsal sessions outside
class.

The student directors learn to conduct these rehearsals during the immediately preceding unit (often on *Peer Gynt*), when I lead the class through
a number of "working rehearsals." Asking for a volunteer cast, I invite the
"audience" to help me direct: we set the scene, plan the blocking, and
discuss character motivation and various superobjectives. As the actors move
through these rehearsal scenes, I frequently stop them, inquiring about the
implications of their particular improvised stage business or their vocal emphases on certain lines. By discussing these specific "directorial" choices,
the students begin to discern the relationship between physical activity and
character motivation on stage: what the actors *do* reveals what the characters
want. As they link the detailed performance choices, they also perceive how
characters' "beats" add up to overall motivations for scenes and, in turn,
create "spines" for the entire script, the contributions of the characters to
the play's action.

To encourage the directors to consider various approaches to the play, I
suggest that they examine the ways in which other directors or critics have
produced or interpreted *A Doll House*. Sprinchorn's disclosure that Ibsen

wanted to cast a "matinee idol" as Torvald (Durbach 120) may lead a director to reappraise a conception of that character, for example. Hurt's description of Nora's "project of the will" as her attempt to preserve her marriage through "deceit and role-playing" (105) may foster a directorial vision that questions Nora's means to her goal. A director may read, say, the *New York Times* review of Ingmar Bergman's 1968 London production of *Hedda Gabler* and decide to use a similar "dual stage" for *A Doll House.* I do not assign particular readings from the standard critical and biographical works on reserve but let the students follow their own interests; this procedure ensures variety in the research and in the directorial approaches. The result of this optional research must be evident in the scene presentation itself, though the director may describe, before the performance, any production elements that could not be secured or readily presented on stage.

To encourage actors to prepare their scene work thoughtfully, I ask for a written account of and justification for each approach to character, an essay due the day of performance. While the actor's analysis concerns motivation and interaction with other characters, the director's essay focuses on the play and the assigned scene as a whole. (See App. at the end of this essay.)

After each scene presentation during the *A Doll House* unit, the class analyzes the director's approach, especially the performance choices the director made—or failed to make—in the scene. The director and actors must be able to articulate and defend their central action for *A Doll House,* for the particular scene, and for each character, as well as their setting, costume, and lighting designs. We discuss whether the script justifies the approach, examine new insights, and determine problems created for character motivation in later scenes.

After the first three of the five scenes have been performed, I require two evening gatherings to view Losey's and Garland's film productions of *A Doll House.* Though students often disagree with both directorial viewpoints, they respond enthusiastically to watching an entire production and can clearly see the performance choices involved. Following the film showings, we debate the merits and weaknesses of the two approaches and compare and contrast them with the class's scene presentations.

I try to guide students toward an understanding of the characters' meta-theatrical or self-dramatizing tendencies—elements central to my vision of the script—which I present as yet another possible approach for us to examine. In the assigned opening scene of act 1, for example, I point out that although Torvald may want to appear the stern disciplinarian, to dramatize himself as the head of the household, he seems as delighted as a child about the prospect of freedom from monetary worries and truly wants to play games with Nora. In an inverse manner, she plays the role of the willful child, while she is actually quite adult in her interaction with the maid and the porter and in her desire to acquire money to repay Krogstad.

Our second scene presentation, the tarantella scene, illustrates the dangers of this self-dramatizing and of casting others in idealized roles. Torvald abets Nora's melodramatic, sacrificial concept of herself as he directs her—and as both of them become dancing Capri dolls. Not even Rank can save Nora, because of his attempt to force her into the theatrical role of deathbed "lover." When Torvald histrionically promises his wife, "I'll be your slave— you sweet, helpless little thing," he follows her lead: he satisfies his desire to be powerful by pretending to be helpless with someone he thinks needs him. But that very pretense strips him of his strength. In contrast, in the third assigned scene, when Krogstad attempts to cast Kristine as the heartless villain and himself as the wronged lover, Kristine retains their joint power by refusing to play the role.

The young couple's return from the party and Rank's farewell, which follows in the next scene presentation, multiplies Nora's personas. Torvald first casts Nora as the lovely Capri dancer who must exit on cue, then as his virginal bride, and finally as his wife, dangerous and in danger. Nora, how- ever, demands her cue for a different role: she reminds Torvald to read his mail. Then, curiously, she takes time to don Torvald's coat, yet another costume. She stalls for time not only for the pleasure of witnessing Torvald's enactment of her romantic vision of him as savior but also in an unconscious attempt to affirm that part of herself that can indeed save her—and perhaps Torvald. If "male" and "female" identities can fuse within Nora and within Torvald, the metatheatrical roles they have been playing might collapse.

Of course, Torvald's stormy entrance and Nora's final change of costume in preparation for her exit signal the apparent impossibility of this solution. To generate discussion following this last scene presentation, I quote Ibsen's debatable speech to the League for Women's Rights: "It is women who shall solve the human problem. As mothers they shall solve it. And only in that capacity can they solve it" (Sprinchorn, *Ibsen: Letters* 338). I also encourage students to consider the possibility that Nora's view of Torvald as a savior is as debilitating as his conception of her as a doll-child.

The performance approach I have outlined helps students discover the complexities of Ibsen's drama, the histrionics as well as the heroism of Nora and Torvald. But it also presents them with an aesthetic experience that is qualitatively different from a "poetic" approach. By collaborating with Ibsen to direct, design, and perform *A Doll House*, students can perceive all the elements of the script's semiotic system simultaneously. They learn to hear and see Nora, to discern the implied oral and visual cues in the dialogue. Excited about their newly developing critical skills, they enjoy learning about drama in this fashion. On a practical level, the method engages them as directly as possible in the analytical-creative production process and lends variety and a specific focus to each class meeting. But most important, the method "knows" more than any single practitioner: each student scene presentation challenges and refines my own reading of *A Doll House*.

Appendix

Scene Analysis: Director
Duties:
- Act as artistic leader for the group producing the scene.
- Schedule rehearsal times and arrange for a rehearsal hall.
- Before the first rehearsal, reread the play at least once, and answer the questions below for yourself, so that you can lead your group to an enactment of the scene *as you see it*. On the day of your scene presentation, hand in an essay answering these questions. Also turn in a written account of rehearsal times and attendance at rehearsals.
  1. What is your vision of the play? (What is it about? What is its central action?) Defend your view against other possible approaches. Cite textual support.
  2. What is the primary action in this scene?
  3. Why is this particular scene included in the play?
  4. Where and when does this scene take place? Why? Describe the setting, lighting, costuming, and any special effects you would create if you had production funds. How do they help reveal your idea of the play?

Scene Analysis: Actor
Duties:
- Make the character's actions clear to the class.
- Attend *all* rehearsals *promptly*.
- Provide a costume or suggestion of costume for your character.
- Before the first rehearsal, reread the play at least once, then examine the assigned scene carefully. On the day of your scene presentation, hand in your written scene analysis. To complete the analysis, first photocopy your scene, and on the copy, note the following:
  1. On the top of the first page, write down what you consider the character's main action in the scene (use the phrase "to do what?").
  2. In the text, put a slash mark each time your character's action changes. Be precise about when one action stops and another begins, and number each new section as you create it.
  3. In the margins, or on a separate sheet, write down what you think your action is for each individual section or "beat." Be certain that you clarify which action goes with which section of the scene: use corresponding numbers.

4. Remember that your character's action begins as the scene opens and is not necessarily tied to his or her lines. A nonspeaking character also has motivations that may change from moment to moment. Your character's motivation may change during a silence or someone else's speech.

5. On a separate sheet, type a justification for the choices you've made. Answer the following questions: What is your character's action in this scene? in the play? What support does the script offer for your approach? How does your choice enrich your character and other characters in the play? Defend your choice against other possible approaches to the character. Were any of your preferred choices squelched by the director's view of the scene or squashed by technical difficulties?

Definitions:
- *The action of the play* is its overall movement, its "superobjective"; it should be stated in an infinitive phrase.
- *A character's action* is his or her motivation, or "spine"; the reason the character does something (stated in an infinitive phrase).
- *Behavior* is stage business or physical activity; the visible or audible manifestations of the character's action or of the character's attempt to camouflage an action.
- *Sample actions*:
  Wrong: to be indifferent (merely describes a state; does not propel character or cite reason for behavior).
  Wrong: to express surprise (describes behavior, not an action. An action tells why the character does something. He or she could express surprise to cover up guilt, to flirt with a spouse, or for many other reasons).
  Right: Act 2 RANK: Oh, you won't miss me long! Those who go away—are soon forgotten.
  NORA: (*Looks at him anxiously.*) You really believe that?
  On Nora's line the action might be "to mull over and try to reject the possibility that Torvald won't miss her after she has sacrificed herself to protect him."

Creating *A Doll House* from Life

David Downs

In a three-year acting course that covers actor training from the basic inner techniques to the principles of style and audience communication, early work on characterization begins in the first quarter with the study of human behavior through sensory perception. Students work to analyze character not through the intellect but through detailed study of actual behavior, through the senses' perception of human responses to the specific stimuli of the environment. Students are expected to know selected plays of Shakespeare, Shaw, Chekhov, and Ibsen in order to apply their work directly to dramatic characterization. The goal is to develop the actor's capacity to perceive human behavior meaningfully rather than simply to observe and to imitate indiscriminately.

Each sense is studied individually, following this pattern (for the sense of touch): (1) Start with yourself: What do your hands reveal about you? In response to what stimuli do your hands reveal "student"? What if you were a banker? a father? Torvald Helmer? (2) Study someone you know: What do my hands do that reveal "actor"? "teacher"? What if your hands responded as mine do? Create a characterization of me through the sense of touch. (3) Dramatic character: How do Rank's hands reveal "doctor"? Demonstrate. Now let the doctor's hands touch Nora's silk stocking. What happens? Why? Create Torvald through his sense of touch: Torvald writes a check; Torvald greets his son, his daughter; Torvald ties a ribbon in Nora's hair.

To experience the kinesthetic sense, the muscle sense, most directly, students study animals at the zoo and bring their observations to class; they study a child's response to fireworks, the seashore, a Christmas tree. Then: Become a wild stallion; what motivates a stallion? Then add an opposing force: What if it were corralled? Transfer to drama: Hedda Gabler's kinesthetic responses are constrained. Show with your spine and muscles that Hedda wants to ride a horse wildly, but she sits erect on her Victorian sofa. Nora's kinesthetic sense is still as active as a child's. Become Nora selecting a surprise Christmas present for Torvald and then dance in delight. What happens to Nora's kinesthetic responsiveness by the end of the play? Why?

The work does not yet focus on the plays as plays; rather I concentrate on human behavior and encourage students to study characters in sensory detail while observing real human beings. They read Stanislavski's texts and Boleslavski's *Acting: The First Six Lessons*. The class is asked not to do specific exercises from the books but to search for what the artists were getting at and to devise their own illustrations of the principles. Students keep daily journals to record their work outside class. My written comments in each journal tailor assignments to individual student progress; if a student needs more work to develop the ability to perceive through hearing, I might make suggestions such as these: Listen to voices. Note their effects on your muscles, your spine. What quality soothes? grates? invigorates? Listen to the man sitting next to you. What specific vocal qualities reveal the steeled, determined voice of a Krogstad? Let your voice become this real-life Krogstad's. Can you get to the human source of such a voice, to the motivation behind such vocal expression, to the why behind the how? Why is Krogstad not simply a melodrama villain? Find the answer not in intellectual or psychological terms but in terms of your body's understanding.

When such suggestions lead to discovery, I follow up: What is the difference between Nora's voice and Kristine's? Why? Demonstrate for the class. Nora hears a Norwegian folk song (go to the library and do research). Krogstad hears the same song. Dr. Rank hears it. What do you learn about each from their responses? Students record their work processes and resulting discoveries in the journals; they bring the outside world into the classroom and apply what they know about living human beings to the living characters of drama. To this end, I ask them to study the notebooks of Leonardo da Vinci and Chekhov. Class time is designed to give direction and clarification to their work, to offer further illustrations and active suggestions, but the real work of discovering and training perceptive human totality takes place outside the classroom walls and gets recorded in the actor's daily notebook.

As their ability to perceive develops, students look for life models of the characters. Have you perceived Nora in a sorority sister as she dresses for a special date? Show the class in specific detail. Have you ever coaxed a boyfriend into changing a movie date to a study date? Recreate for the class. Following such demonstration, there are more questions: Now that you've watched Ann recreate herself cajoling her father into letting her stay up late so that she could finish knitting his birthday sweater in secret, what specific responses revealed Nora? How does Nora's capacity to keep a secret reveal itself in her eyes? her spine? her laughter? What reveals Nora's capacity to reason? to get to the Nora who slams the door?

My response to such work includes discussions of the play, the specifics of nineteenth-century Norway, Ibsen's themes, and so forth. These discussions may lead to my sending students to the library for Lucy Barton's *Historic Costume for the Stage* and to the local historical museum to study actual clothing of the period. Sensory perception and human behavior are kept at the fore, however; the actor's essential ability is the capacity to translate any idea, any concept, into terms of actual illustrative behavioral response. I might suggest to the women, get a bustle and a full-length dress from the costume shop. What happens to the way you move? Which muscles are involved? What are the differences from contemporary clothing? Note the alterations in your perceptions of the world. Sing a Christmas carol and dance for Torvald. Similarly, the men discover Torvald in starched collars and tight suits and silk hats. They go to the Art Institute to study furniture of the period, then use specific responses to turn a rehearsal chair into a wingback chair, a wooden box into a tiled stove, and so on.

As they begin to learn the importance of perception and life study for understanding human motivation and character, students expand their training in the second quarter toward developing the actor's creative imagination. While the classwork covers too varied a range of topics to describe in detail here, the essential organizing assignment may give an idea of this quarter's objective. Students study novels of character; for example, *Anna Karenina*, *The Return of the Native*, *Madame Bovary*. Novels provide specific elements of environment and period and detailed descriptions of the total response of human beings to their situations: what characters do as they speak that reveals the whole truth of their response as words alone cannot; what characters are thinking but not revealing in words; what associations and preoccupations play on characters as they respond with all senses to significant stimuli.

Students apply what they learn from the novels to the plays they are studying. Read the passage in which Anna Karenina is introduced. On stage, can you create in actual human behavior what Tolstoy creates in words? Then: Write Nora's entrance as though it were a passage from a novel. Include all significant details of response that Ibsen cannot provide in the playscript. In the classroom present the passage on stage in action. What have you learned? Apply your knowledge to Christine entering Nora's home, to the scene between Nora and Dr. Rank.

From the work on the novels, students learn to read plays for clues to creating what the dramatist imagined. What do character names reveal? (Of "Gabler" and "Tesman" which is the bourgeois name? Which the upper-class name? What are the implications for behavior? Manifestations in the play?) What does the title touch off in your imagination? (Why is *A Doll House* a more appropriate translation than *A Doll's House*?) The use of metaphor? (Become a lark hopping from branch to branch, singing outside a bedroom window. Transfer to Nora when Torvald comes home from the bank.) Significant objects? (Of all the activities Ibsen could have chosen for Nora, why the eating of macaroons?) Occasion? (Why Christmas?) Specific setting, time of day, order in which characters are introduced? And always the students' work takes the form of action and improvisation, of thinking and analyzing in terms of the senses instead of the mind. The work encourages the student to think of the actor as a novelist in action terms, translating ideas into communicative human behavior as the novelist translates ideas into communicative words.

Spring quarter focuses the work on perception and the work on imagination into the specific work of characterization. What is human character? How does it emerge from a background of complex forces—social and economic forces, inherited traits, nationality, political and religious influences, personal factors of health, age, sex, occupation, education? The aim of this quarter's work is to create, in terms of human response to stimuli, the specific forces from whose dynamics the characters of a play develop.

Students keep detailed workbooks of sources: traditional sources from the library, trips to the Norwegian Consulate and the Chicago Norwegian Society, historical accounts, music of the period, art, literature, political pamphlets, photographs—anything that contributes to their grasp of what makes up the world of the play. Equally important are today's newspaper and magazine stories that illustrate the concerns of the play as they manifest themselves in contemporary life: the world of *A Doll House* exists in the present. The students are attempting to discover in human terms the conflicting social forces that form the active basis of human needs, drives, motivations—character.

The world of *A Doll House* is a man's world: man is the breadwinner who provides and protects, who creates an environment in which the woman can flourish as wife and mother. Only the man needs to worry about financial, legal, and business matters. The woman plays with the children, delights her husband, entertains friends. Men play the tune and women dance to it, to the utter delight of all. Beneath this world lie opposing and determining forces: the need to discover the self versus the need to play according to spoken and unspoken rules; living in ignorance of the laws of society versus being judged according to those laws; playing a role perfectly versus discovering one's potential as an individual human being.

Both historical period material and current contemporary accounts are always translated into improvised situations. Working improvisationally leads students to discover basic drives of character, relationships among characters, and conflicting forces that best dramatize the play's themes. Nora becomes a vital, lovely young woman, motivated to please Torvald, to dance, to sing; with it all, she has the capacity to reason, to question, to break through the surface of her life should circumstances ever become extreme enough to force such a realization. Torvald is a loving, doting husband, a charming and confident young man making his way in a man's world of business, a world in which appearances are crucial to happiness, in which a wife lives a happy delightful life at home. And they are real people responding to a real world, not simply characters in a play.

The overall objective behind the first year's diversity of work is to get students thinking, demonstrating, working actively and imaginatively to create the human reality of the people and the situations of any drama. Students must learn to avoid the easy intellectual grasp, to get to comprehension in the senses and the muscles, to involve the total human self, which is the actor's artistic medium. The actor must know not only how to talk about a play but also how to create it.

In the second year students focus on the plays as drama, studying Greek tragedy, Shakespeare, Chekhov, Shaw, Ibsen. Formal lectures are supplemented by weekly essays from me with comments on class work, suggestions for further reading, and other important matters that cannot be covered in class. Scenes are studied not as isolated units but as dramatized selections of an organic whole. Students are taught to see themselves as studying not simply "acting" but rather drama and theater from the actor's point of view. Work is always kept in progress, nothing is set, the spontaneity of improvisation is maintained. I work concurrently on stage with students, guiding, prodding, providing actual physical stimuli and motivation, not just verbal observations from the back of the room. The daily journal this year becomes a record of work done in preparation for class presentation. Students learn to create character, relationships, environment, situation, and conflict as these elements manifest themselves in the specific incidents dramatized in the play; they learn to build sequences, to mark climaxes, to create the contrasting rhythms of the play. Class discussion always leads students back to the stage to illustrate in active terms the ideas generated.

For the unit on Ibsen, required reading includes Eric Bentley's *The Playwright as Thinker*, Maurice Valency's *The Flower and the Castle*, Robert Brustein's *The Theater of Revolt*, Francis Fergusson's *The Idea of a Theatre*, and selected chapters from Michael Meyer's biography. I assign papers in which students discuss aspects of each playwright's work not from the academic point of view (ideas) but from the actor's point of view (human behavior as illustrative of ideas). The final paper is a character analysis in conjunction with the final class presentation:

1. State in literal action terms Ibsen's objectives, the theme of the play, Ibsen's point of view on the theme.
2. What character traits are determined by the theme?
3. Analyze environmental influences, determining factors of character; discuss resulting emotional, mental, physical behavior patterns, vocal patterns, and so on.
4. Discuss relationships with other characters, their manifestations.
5. Discuss the language of the play, the imagery, the prosodic structure, the prose rhythms, with relation to character.
6. Discuss character development or lack of development.

In the third year, students turn to the final phase of the actor's creative work—style. They learn how to select a response from the myriad improvised responses, heighten and intensify reality, orchestrate all elements, sharpen their timing, point up significant details—all the techniques that give created realities entertainment value, form, and meaning.

The first quarter is designed to illustrate style as an artistic process. We spend several class periods on novels, music, and painting in an effort to discover the principles of style that underlie all art. Then students do comparative studies from drama: Arrange the furniture on stage in a typical Ibsen room. Now show us a Chekhov room. What is the difference? What are the implications for the general themes of the plays? Which room will have a more lived-in feeling? How is this feeling achieved? How is Ibsen's concern with the double standard revealed? Which is the more class-conscious society?

Next students may create representative servants from Chekhov, Ibsen, Shakespeare, Molière. What kinds of activities does each engage in naturally? How do they interact with employers? What are the implications about the thematic concerns of the playwrights? I may have students show servants changing scenery between acts. What is appropriate for Ibsen but not for Shakespeare? Why? Written assignments focus on the questions, What is style for the actor? How is the playwright's theme revealed through characters, dramatic situations, play construction? Since it is the playwright's point of view on the theme that determines the particular process of selection and emphasis of detail that we call style, what clues do you discover toward embodying that point of view?

In the second quarter, students apply to realism the principles they discovered in the first quarter. On their own they create character, relationships, environment, situation, and conflict, which were the focus of the previous year's study. They bring their work to class, which now emphasizes the principles of audience communication. Perhaps they design Krogstad's entrance during Nora's game with her children. Exactly what story do you want to tell? in what order? by what specific details of behavior? Often students write the details in the form of a simple step-by-step list: (1) A knock at the door (loud? rapid? tentative? why?). (2) The children see Nora under the table, run to her laughing. (3) Louder knocking. (4) Nora chases Bob, runs past the door. (5) Door opens a crack. (6) Nora catches Bob, they tumble to the floor. (7) Krogstad's head appears; he steps into full view, straightens his spine, removes his hat (?). (8) "Beg pardon . . ." (9) Nora shrieks, freezes, turns. In class we work on the sequence of actions, testing and adjusting until we discover the clearest, most logical sequence of telling Ibsen's story.

After working in class, the actors go off with a student director to incorporate the new material. The second time the scene is done, I continue to work on stage with both the actors and the director. Was character truthfully created and clearly manifested? Were relationships established clearly? Did interplay proceed honestly? Were sequences built logically? Were climaxes capped? Was the dramatic point of the scene made strongly? Does each detail of action take the play logically one step closer to the slamming of the door?

Each scene is brought in a third time as a finished work. I do not interrupt with suggestions or work ideas. It is a performance. The discussion afterward focuses on the audience. Did the audience experience the entertaining joy of discovery with each moment? Did they respond to each moment as the play wishes them to? Be specific. Were they carried along easily, willingly, logically? Did the action proceed with suspense and with inevitability? In other words, did the presentation have style?

The actor's job is to translate ideas and concepts into details of human behavior, to illustrate through simple truthful sensory response the thematic concerns behind character and situation and conflict in a play. Guided by the perspective of the playwright's point of view, actors cast their created realities into theatrical form so that every detail, every response, will lead the audience logically, inevitably, artistically to the slamming of the door, to the confused Torvald sitting helpless at the table, and ultimately to a fuller comprehension of what *A Doll House* can mean for human beings in contemporary life.

THE GRADUATE COURSE

A *Doll House*; or, The Fortunate Fall

Brian Johnston

My goal in teaching *A Doll House* (or any other Ibsen play) is to get students to see that Ibsen's realism depends on a metaphoric poetic method that extends the text in depth to the furthest limits of implication. Using the close-reading techniques applied in the study of poetry, I try to encourage the class to respond to the play imaginatively but not to indulge in merely subjective and enthusiastic extensions of the text. To this end I emphasize the objective structure of the play, its discernible pattern of correspondences on which the students and I can agree, and then relate this structure to the texture of the play: its pattern of images, its significant repeating of key words and phrases, and so on. Since the students in my graduate seminar do not know Norwegian, I point out important patterns in the original that are not always present in the translations. I also use extensive background material: Ibsen's letters and speeches, his earlier and later dramas, and other texts, such as M. H. Abrams's study of Romanticism, *Natural Supernaturalism*, that are not usually associated with Ibsen studies. Because the seminar is on the cycle of Ibsen's plays from *Pillars of Society* to *When We Dead Awaken*, *A Doll House* is studied as one part of a unified whole.

Most of the students have already taken my course on Romantic drama, from the pre-Romantic Lessing through Schiller, Goethe, Kleist, Buechner, de Musset, Hugo, the Scribean school, Wagner (*The Ring*), and Ibsen (the earlier plays up to *Emperor and Galilean*). The many theories of Romantic drama, from Lessing (*Hamburg Dramaturgy*) to the writings of Wagner and

Nietzsche (*The Birth of Tragedy*), were also studied in some depth so that the student could see the claims made for the modern theater by Ibsen's predecessors and the "world-view" such a theater was likely to mirror. I believe this preparation is indispensable if one is to arrive at even a partially adequate idea of what Ibsen is up to in the realist cycle. My approach, therefore, is suitable primarily for a graduate class. Central to the approach are the following points:

1. The dialectical action of *A Doll House*, the second work of a twelve-play cycle, evolves out of that of *Pillars of Society* and evolves toward that of *Ghosts*.
2. The play presents the dialectical process whereby an inadequate and false consciousness of reality, shared by the Helmers, is put under pressure and painfully relinquished for a higher level of consciousness.
3. This dialectical requirement shapes the realism, creating those "un-realistic" coincidences and plot symmetries, ironies and fateful juxta-positions, so embarrassing to the slice-of-life interpreters.
4. The dialectical action of the play reactivates the "ghosts"—the arche-types from the spiritual past of the race. This summoning of the old powers of the past to the carefully delimited space and time of Ibsen's stage constitutes the ritualist aspect of his realism that modern produc-tions must discover.

The student fresh from Arthur Miller and the modern drama anthologies would be baffled by this claim for an archetypal and ritualist dimension to Ibsen's realism, but not the student familiar with Romantic art and thought and with Ibsen's writings and plays. Along with my *The Ibsen Cycle*, Walter Kaufmann's translation of Hegel's preface to *The Phenomenology of Mind* is used to demonstrate the nature of the dialectical vision of reality as a con-tinuously restless uncovering and overcoming of contradictions and conflicts within reality. This concept prepares the student for a multilayered texture within Ibsen's plays. I want students to see that Ibsen was a visionary poet of the theater creating ambitious artworks by means of a realism that, as much as Wagner's more overtly symbolic method, employs metaphors for the totality of the human spirit through the details of scene, characters, actions, language, and properties. By emphasizing the way in which the meanings of the plays emerge through their objective details (I discourage speculation on the supposed "inner life" of Nora), I prevent students from making facile attributions of significance.

The ideological structure of the play, in which carefully conceived (and named) characters and histories are placed in significant juxtaposition, gives depth and range of meaning to the frugal seeming terms of *A Doll House* or *Ghosts*. By demonstrating that Torvald and Nora are recreations of Einar and Agnes in the earlier scenes of *Brand*, one can show the similarity of Agnes's and Nora's character transformations while also revealing the extension of the pagan-Christian argument from the earlier play. For Torvald and Nora, an "aesthetic" and "pagan" pair like Einar and Agnes, will have their lives fatefully affected and altered by the "Christian" pair, Christine and Krogstad. Torvald and Nora are names deriving from northern and southern paganism (as are Alving and Helene in *Ghosts*), while the Christian derivation of Christine (Kristine) is self-evident. *Krog*stad has implications of crookedness, deviousness, and deformity, all qualities of Ibsen's "satanic" figures (more physically evident in Engstrand of the next play), while Krogstad's first name, Nils, is a diminutive of Nicholas, the name of the satanic bishop of *The Pretenders* (who actually returns from Hell). None of this would be worth mentioning if it were not that Krogstad is given an eminently satanic role. An illusorily "innocent" pair, in their Eden, the Helmers are menaced by the satanic Krogstad; they undergo a fortunate fall into a knowledge of good and evil, with the help of Christine, Krogstad's partner. After first seeking to *save* the Helmers from Krogstad, she finally decides on tougher terms of salvation—terms requiring the pair to open their souls to truth and mutual reconciliation (a prescription repeated, with even more alarming results, by the messianic Gregers Werle in *The Wild Duck*). My approach clearly makes it impossible to seal off *A Doll House* from the patterns and themes of Ibsen's other work. The student is expected to be familiar with the larger "argument" of the cycle (and of Ibsen's lifework) as well as with the localized form of that argument in the play.

After their expulsion from their Eden of false consciousness, Nora, and eventually Torvald, must journey toward a more adult and adequate, if also more desolate, experience of reality, such as we encounter in *Ghosts*. And Nora, the name of the "central consciousness" of *A Doll House*, is a diminutive of Eleonora, a form of Helene—the name of the central consciousness of *Ghosts*. The teacher should here demonstrate the "expanding circumferences" of the three seismic shocks undergone by Nora's consciousness. In act 1 the shock involves social reality, in act 2 psychological reality, and in act 3 ethical-metaphysical reality. All three shocks are associated with Krogstad (who administers the first two and leaves the protagonists to suffer the third). Thus Krogstad is no mere plot device, instigating Nora's agon; he is integral to the entire ideological, as well as dramatic, structure.

The condition of false consciousness (that one's "innocence" can be uninvolved in the world's evil) is closely bound up with the concept of "the wonderful" (*det vidunderlige*)—a key word for establishing the meaning of the play. This word, too, will undergo social, psychological, and metaphysical forms. In act 1 the wonderful is Torvald's new social position as bank manager and the splendid new material prosperity and freedom it will bring to the pair. In act 2 the wonderful has become a nonmaterialist value: Nora's imagined transformation of the characters into the heroic figures she always believed would emerge from their marriage. Finally, the "most wonderful thing of all" (*det vidunderligste*), which has yet to happen, becomes a project for the spiritual future toward which the couple must separately journey. Here, the teacher must go to the original text, for translations do not always render this careful pattern of repetitions. In each act the word "wonderful" is repeated at least three times in close iteration between two people, and in its superlative form (*det vidunderligste*) it is the triple repetition actually closing the play, like a major theme significantly transposed in a new key at the end of a musical work. The teacher can show that this dialectical evolution of a concept is no merely abstract conflict by having students act out each of its occurrences to note the transformation of meaning that has taken place.

The time the action takes place—Christmas—also indicates the play's ideological structure. The Norwegian word retains the pagan origins of the feast of twelve days (*jol*), and the opening words of act 1, Nora's "Hide the yule tree well," not only introduce the important leitmotiv of hiding and concealment but also, together with the couple's manner of celebrating the season, establish this pagan derivation. The feasting, dancing, and gift giving occupy their thoughts, not the more solemn Christian themes, which they never mention. But the sorrow and guilt associated with the Christian consciousness will invade the house in the figures of Christine and Krogstad. In both pagan and Christian traditions, this time of year marks the death of the old and the birth of the new, materially and spiritually. In act 1 Torvald and Nora, in their doll home, movingly look forward to the wonderful that is about to happen to them: the brave new material world lying open before them. But this Christmas will bring them more alarming gifts—truth and freedom, those dangerous agents of the third empire.

Immediately after the pair speaks of the wonderful, the door bell rings, bringing Christine, with her contrasting realities of suffering and self-sacrifice, as well as her coincidental involvement, past and present, in the life of the disgraced and menacing Krogstad. The teacher should demonstrate these coincidences to be intentional and significant, like the strong irony. Advancing beyond the consciousness of *Pillars of Society*, Torvald acknowledges that "evil" exists in his community but believes he can aesthetically quarantine his dollhouse from contamination. As a lawyer he will not touch "sordid" cases, leaving them to Krogstad, who hardly can touch anything else. Furthermore he intends, in the New Year, to sever all connections with Krogstad by dismissing him from the bank. But Torvald's and Nora's doll innocence is really ignorance, for it is through Krogstad that they will begin to perceive the undetected layers of their own humanity.

Another word cluster should be considered. Nora tells Christine that she desires a life free of sorrow (*sorgløs*), and this word receives quadruple iteration, along with another appearance of "wonderful" in act 1, and, again, the door bell rings, this time to usher in the sorrowful Krogstad. Another man of sorrows, Dr. Rank is a frequent visitor to the house, but both Torvald and Nora aesthetically distance this sorrow so that it actually becomes an agreeably somber background to their "sunlit lives." The student can be sent to the text to discover the numerous references to Torvald as "aesthetic" and to note resemblances to the escapist aesthetics of Einar in *Brand*. Ibsen uses Krogstad's moral darkness to set off to better effect the purity of the doll home. But, it can be demonstrated, Nora also conspires in this escapist ploy and in one of the play's strongest scenes (in act 2) tries to prevent Rank from describing his approaching death and his love for her. She does not want the "foreground" of her consciousness invaded by such realities, for she is just now creating the fantasies of Torvald's and her heroism. But it is Nora whom we first see facing up to sorrowful truth, which she hears from both Rank and Krogstad.

Students can be alerted to a parallel between financial credit and moral credit, both involving Krogstad. By hiring Christine and dismissing Krogstad, Torvald precipitates the crisis that will reveal that, in Ibsen's metaphysics, you don't get your Christine without your Krogstad. By conveniently representing the evil of the world on which Torvald can so complacently expatiate, Krogstad has allowed the Helmers to live off a false fund of virtue; thus his insistence on recouping is just, if brutal. For, in the past, he has had to pay the cost of disgrace and ostracism at the hands of virtuous society. Torvald deplores to Nora the harmful effects of this disgrace on Krogstad's children, but neither he nor Nora reflects that the cruel virtue that inflicted it must bear responsibility for the result.

This severance of virtue from evil leads to a drastic loss of self-knowledge on the part of the virtuous. Torvald's boast that his home is free of moral guilt is as vain as his boast that it is free of financial debt (students should be told that Norwegian employs the same word, *skyld*, for both guilt and debt); furthermore, this great ignorance leaves him utterly vulnerable when the great shock arrives.

Torvald remains in his illusory world until the last act, whereas Nora has felt this world dissolve beneath her feet from the moment she and Krogstad had their confrontation. The teacher should point out the social terms of her first shock, which she receives when she discovers that, in the eyes of society (the law), she is as much a criminal as the disgraced Krogstad, however thoughtlessly she committed her crime. Thoughtlessness, my students know from *Peer Gynt*, is the worst defense to plead at Ibsen's judgment day on the soul. By being made, almost for the first time, to consider seriously actions done thoughtlessly, Nora is being forced along a path of self-discovery: an evolution, within one play, that the seminar traces throughout the twelve-play cycle.

Her psychological evolution is revealed in act 2. It is prepared for by her conversation, in the darkening living room, with Rank, and students should be alerted to the parallels between this scene and the later one with Krogstad. Though she desperately attempts to prevent Rank from infiltrating his dark reality into her consciousness, she does commiserate with him, in another word cluster, saying that it is sorrowful (*sørgelig*) that the good (material) things of life should strike at one's bones—and most sorrowful (*sørgeligste*) that they should strike at the bones of those who did not enjoy the fun. Even a careless (*sorgløs*) hedonism nevertheless creates what is sorrowful for the next generation.

In the other scene of sorrow, with Krogstad, Nora and the social outcast confide their mutual cowardice, their failure at the critical moment to find the courage for suicide. This is a shocked discovery not about the world, as in act 1, but about one's self, one's inner spirit, and students have to understand the difference if they are to grasp the dialectic of the play. Dwelling on the depth of this shock, getting the class to discuss it, will make more plausible Nora's resolution at the end of the play, just as Krogstad's "change of heart" can be shown from the text to be no melodramatic conversion of the "villain."

Thus it is essential to demonstrate the increased inwardness of Nora's agitation in act 2—the fear of retribution, a fearfully glimpsed redemption, and a semiecstatic discovery of the courage for suicide. Nora's feelings are expressed in the return of the word "wonderful," again in triple iteration, in her dialogue with Christine. But now the wonderful is also the "terrible" (*forferdelig*), which must not be allowed to happen, "not for anything in the world" (Fjelde's trans.). For it will be the spectacle of Torvald heroically destroying himself for Nora's sake and of Nora, to prevent that, taking her own life. In this fantasy the doll pair have become Tristan and Isolde, and in anticipation of this sublime and terrible destiny Nora wildly dances the tarantella "as if her life were at stake." Students should note that Nora has already evolved considerably into a "romantic" heroine but that she still has a process of evolution to undergo.

The symmetry of the plot (revealing its thematic, ideological content) can be demonstrated from act 3, in which the round table is moved to the center of the living room. At it, one couple will sit to talk of past and present, to unite; another will sit to talk of past and present, to separate. This symmetry can be depicted on the blackboard by the following diagram:

Act 1   Act 3

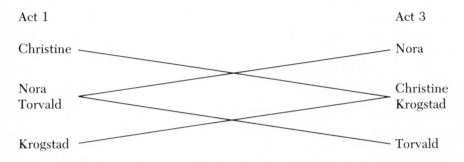

Christine ———————————————————————— Nora

Nora ———————————————————————— Christine
Torvald   Krogstad

Krogstad ———————————————————————— Torvald

Nils and Christine, after long sorrow, unite in great joy. Torvald and Nora, like Einar and Agnes before they meet Brand, are dancing in false joy on the heights but will descend to sorrow—and to truth and to the possibility of freedom. The most wonderful thing of all, which alone can unite them again, is a more heroic—and more pagan—value than Nils's and Christine's sorrow and repentance modulating into joy; it is far beyond the "wonderful" of acts 1 and 2. Those had been the projects of the still childish Nora, but now both Torvald and Nora must put away all childish things (the theme of the title of the play) for something like a new metaphysics for living: the "third empire" that Ibsen always insisted was what he sought to foster by his writing.

In these few pages I obviously cannot show how I flesh out this ideological structure of the play with rich human and theatrical detail. But a grasp of the ideological structure, of the argument of the play, helps the teacher to make the wealth of detail coherent and significant, as well as to relate the play to Ibsen's lifework. During my semester-long seminar we discuss how Ibsen achieves a uniquely effective theatrical realism, where the magical coincidences and ironies, the metaphors and symbols, are thrilling manifestations of spirit within reality and not stagey flaws in the artist's search for photographic verisimilitude. Those on-cue ringings of door bells or knocks at the door, and the gathering together of such fateful characters and events in one confined space, become powers created by the theater-magician's spell. Ibsen's famous invaders of closed-off and complacent spaces—Lona Hessel, Christine Linde, Gregers Werle, the Stranger, Hilde Wangel, the Rat Wife—are these not the heralds, or hierophants, of painful but liberating mysteries?

A *Doll House* in a Graduate Seminar

Richard Hornby

In my seminar on Ibsen, the focus is always on the individual play text. I hope that the play will open itself up to us, that we will be startled as its deeper meanings are revealed. I say "us" and "we" because I believe that a good seminar is a fresh experience for everybody, including the professor. For this to happen requires that, first, students thoroughly prepare themselves by doing background reading; second, the professor guides the discussion by asking carefully chosen questions about key elements in the play; and, third, the professor pays close attention to students' answers, participates in the discussion, and follows up with further questions invented extemporaneously.

A seminar professor is like an improvisational actor. Good improvisational acting is never just laissez-faire; it is always based on a strong framework of situation, locale, and character. The performance itself requires an exceptional alertness and a sense of relaxed ease, as the actor picks up minute clues from his or her partners that suggest interesting ways to proceed. Similarly, the seminar professor must provide a strong framework (of background reading, analytical methods, and clear goals) but at the same time must "live the part," responding to what is actually happening in class, instead of just reciting ideas previously discovered. For this reason, it is often difficult to lead a seminar on a topic one has extensively lectured on or written about; old truths, no matter how valid, cannot by themselves bring a seminar to life.

In the sections below, I suggest both preparatory background reading for a seminar on Ibsen and specific questions for discussions on *A Doll House*. I also suggest some ways to follow up on these questions, but again, success here depends on the professor's ability to improvise. It helps if the professor rereads the play thoroughly, no more than twenty-four hours before the class meets, no matter how many times one has read or taught the play before; every detail is instantly recallable. In addition, it is important to spend a half hour or so beforehand going over one's notes, not to rehearse what one will say, but rather to enter into a relaxed, interested mood. One should try here to find some new things about the play, looking particularly at parts one has never taught before. Then, it is a good idea to get to the class a little early and to chat with the students as they come in. This will help put everyone in a good frame of mind to proceed.

Background Reading and General Format

In my seminar we cover all Ibsen's plays from *Brand* forward—a total of sixteen plays, which is about right for a one-semester seminar that closely examines most of them. I divide the plays into four periods: Romanticism (*Brand, Peer Gynt, The League of Youth, Emperor and Galilean*), Social Realism (*Pillars of Society, A Doll House, Ghosts, An Enemy of the People*), Psychological Realism (*The Wild Duck, Rosmersholm, The Lady from the Sea, Hedda Gabler*), and Expressionism (*The Master Builder, Little Eyolf, John Gabriel Borkman, When We Dead Awaken*). At the same time, I stress that the plays are united by common themes, character types, and conflicts. That *A Doll House* can be categorized as social realism does not mean that it is a simple thesis piece but, rather, reflects that in this period Ibsen was using social problems as vehicles for the larger themes that always obsessed him: freedom, idealism, validity, crisis, transformation.

The plays in the final three periods are available in a fine, single edition translated by Rolf Fjelde. Fjelde also has available an excellent verse translation of *Peer Gynt*, while *Brand* is available in a British translation by Michael Meyer, who has also written a superb biography of Ibsen. For the kind of close study that we do in the seminar, students should have their own copies of the plays; I encourage them to annotate their texts liberally with questions and comments. Unfortunately, *The League of Youth* and *Emperor and Galilean* are not in print in English; I therefore assign James W. McFarlane's *The Oxford Ibsen*, which is put on reserve in the library. The edition should be put on reserve in any case, since it is noted for its accuracy of translation and its thoroughness—it even includes Ibsen's early drafts, which often make for interesting comparisons with the final versions. I recommend that the students also read some of Ibsen's early plays on their own, in *The Oxford Ibsen*. *Brand* is, after all, Ibsen's eleventh play, and some of the previous ones (especially *The Pretenders*) are quite good; I start with *Brand* partly because texts for earlier plays are unavailable but mostly because, paired with *Peer Gynt*, it provides a strong beginning to the course, establishing the prototype characters and situations that can then be followed through from play to play.

I put quite a bit of other material on reserve. We have been blessed in the past few decades with a number of fine critical studies in English on Ibsen, which dispel the once popular view of him as a simplistic pamphleteer. These studies include M. C. Bradbrook's *Ibsen the Norwegian*, Brian Johnston's *The Ibsen Cycle*, James Kerans's "Kindermord and Will in *Little Ejolf*," G. Wilson Knight's *Henrik Ibsen*, Charles R. Lyons's *Ibsen: The Divided Consciousness*, and John Northam's *Ibsen: A Critical Study*. We do not discuss these works directly, but at the beginning of the seminar I go over the list and describe the thrust of each book. The students can refer to this information later as needed, particularly for their term papers.

As additional background reading, to be discussed during the first few weeks of class, I assign Henry D. Aiken's *The Age of Ideology*, and *Camille and Other Plays*, edited by Stephen S. Stanton. Both are available in cheap paperback editions. The Aiken book gives a brief overview of some of the philosophers affecting Ibsen: Schopenhauer, Hegel, Comte, Mill, Spencer, Kierkegaard, Nietzsche. It helps students to identify Ibsen's style of thought, which is more idealistic and formalized than that of playwrights today. Furthermore, I place on reserve Kierkegaard's *Either/Or* and *Fear and Trembling*, since Kierkegaard's terminology of the developing individual turns out to be helpful in understanding Ibsen's characterizations, particularly in his middle-period plays like *A Doll House*.

The Stanton anthology includes the editor's excellent introduction on the well-made play, the techniques of which—suppressed secrets, exposition, letters and other devices, fortuitous entrances and exits, central misunderstandings, obligatory scene of final confrontation—were all exploited by Ibsen. The students read some of the plays in the anthology—Scribe's *The Glass of Water* and Sardou's *A Scrap of Paper*—to see how hack playwrights of the nineteenth century wrote; the students can thus appreciate how Ibsen adapted their techniques for more serious purposes. Also in the anthology is a thesis play—Augier's *Olympe's Marriage*—and again, Ibsen was able to develop the standard thesis play, with its safe bourgeois moral, into something different and startling.

After several weeks of background reading, we are prepared to read Ibsen's plays. This we do in the order already mentioned, spending perhaps an hour discussing a minor play like *Pillars of Society* and several hours on a major one like *A Doll House*. (It is a good idea to be flexible, however; a seminar can catch fire—or fail to!—at unexpected places.) With the background reading (including Ibsen's previous plays) providing a guide, we explore the structure of each play, finding out what is actually going on, what makes the play work. I urge the students to consider all the characters, rather than only the central ones; to note symbolic rather than only realistic elements; to be sensitive to detail, over which Ibsen's control is often striking; and to be especially aware of theatrical elements like properties, costuming, and setting, since Ibsen's experience as a theater director made him conscious of the expressive powers of physical staging.

Questions and Follow-up

Question 1: How much feminism is in A Doll House? This question is a good icebreaker because of the reputation of the play and because of the topicality of feminism today. It is also a good seminar question, because arguments can be made both for and against the play's being feminist. Those who argue the feminist side will cite Nora's plight as doll child and doll wife, her status in a society that does not acknowledge women as intelligent or independent. Those on the opposite side will point out that feminism itself is never mentioned in the play and that major nineteenth-century feminist issues like votes for women never come up at all. Nora herself shows no interest in social issues throughout most of the play, and even at the end she is interested in changing herself, not society. I like to play devil's advocate in following up this question, taking the side opposite to the tendency of the class. If the tendency is toward feminism, I might point out that there is another woman in the play, Mrs. Linde, who *is* independent and who seems to function extremely well in this society that supposedly stifles women. If the antifeminist side seems to be carrying the day, I might cite some specific lines that show the opposite. What, for example, could be more feminist than Nora's response to Torvald when, in act 3, he maintains that no one sacrifices honor for love? She retorts, "Millions of women have done just that" (Fjelde's trans.). I also point out that the forgery on which the action centers would never even have been necessary if a wife could borrow money without her husband's or father's consent. It is just such unfairness that leads Nora finally to begin questioning her society at the end of the play:

> I find out, for one thing, that the law's not at all what I'd thought— but I can't get it through my head that the law is fair. A woman hasn't a right to protect her dying father or save her husband's life! I can't believe that.

The key to running a discussion is to bring students back to the text. This is particularly important here because the volatility of the issue of feminism can cause the discussion to go astray. Although I have no objection to students learning about feminism, or to their having strong opinions on the subject, my goal is to have them learn something about Ibsen's play. Students need to understand that feminism in *A Doll House*, while definitely important, is not the only, or even the central, concern of the play, which is not a social pamphlet but a subtle, intensely detailed, vivid work of literature.

Question 2: How does Ibsen use the form of the well-made play? This is again an open-ended question. As Cary M. Mazer points out in a separate essay in this book, critics are divided on the subject of the influence of the well-made play on Ibsen. On the one hand, a device like the letter in the mailbox in *A Doll House* is a bit of well-made play trickery, like Scribe's glass of water or Sardou's piece of paper, but on the other hand, note how Ibsen treats it: when Krogstad, in act 3, decides to call the letter back, Mrs. Linde tells him not to, because "this dreadful secret has to be aired; those two have to come to a full understanding." The audience thus knows, in the next scene, that even if Nora succeeds in keeping the letter from Torvald, it will make no difference, since Mrs. Linde will find some other way of airing the dreadful secret. The letter device is "deconstructed," disturbing the audience's expectations and thus calling into question some of their assumptions about moral behavior.

In the same vein, the famous final discussion scene is actually the obligatory scene of confrontation found at the end of well-made plays, but Ibsen deconstructs this convention also. The first two acts present confrontations between Nora, the heroine, and Krogstad, the ostensible villain; nineteenth-century audiences would have thus expected a climactic confrontation between them in the final act, in which Nora would at last triumph and Krogstad would be defeated or morally converted. Instead, Krogstad sees the error of his ways before Nora even arrives on stage in act 3—in other words, one scene too early!—and the final confrontation is instead with her husband, who turns out to be the true "villain" of the piece.

Thus the initial question on the use of the well-made play form should evoke quick and obvious responses; in the follow-up, however, the discussion becomes more interesting, as students explore how Ibsen varies the standard patterns. While hack playwrights like Scribe and Sardou write to a formula, Ibsen subtly alters that formula, manipulating his audience's expectations to force them to reexamine their assumptions.

Question 3: How does Ibsen use theatrical elements in A Doll House? This is not an ambiguous question like the two preceding ones, but it does lead to a rich area of exploration and offers a good change of pace. I have asked the students initially to catalog Ibsen's use of properties, costuming, sound effects, and setting as they read the play; when I get to this question they are usually bursting with answers. The follow-up should then stress the significance of the theatrical elements, relating them to the play's overall meanings.

With regard to properties, students note immediately the delightful business with the macaroons in act 1 (reinforcing our sense of Nora as a character driven by appetite rather than principle), or the erotic use of the silk stockings in act 2, or the contrast between the brightly decorated Christmas tree in act 1 and the same tree in act 2—"stripped of ornament, burned-down candle stubs on its ragged branches"—as the awful moment of discovery approaches. In the same vein, Ibsen has the flirtation scene between Nora and Dr. Rank in act 2 begin in dim light; when Nora's strategy fails and the spell is broken, a lamp is brought in, changing the mood for the audience as well as for the characters. Again and again, reality tends to intrude visually onto the stage, like the tarantella dance that erupts into the staid living room at the end of act 2. *A Doll House* is an extremely visual play, which is one of the reasons it has played so well in translation, into dozens of languages.

As to costuming, we discuss the contrast between Nora's tarantella costume and the sedate, confining costumes the characters ordinarily wear. This disparity is related to the larger irony of the masked ball in act 3, so appropriate in a play concerning characters who must keep up facades—Nora and her forgery, Krogstad and his loan sharking, Torvald's crass nature, Dr. Rank's illness (resulting from his father's scandalous sexual escapades), all hidden behind a masquerade of false propriety, or, in Nora's case, of a brainless coquettishness. Critics have long noted the visual effectiveness of Nora's changing out of her masquerade costume before her departure at the end, symbolizing her inner transformation; for her, the masquerading is over.

The most famous theatrical element of all, of course, is the final door slam as Nora walks out on her husband, but I point out how carefully Ibsen establishes it: the setting produces a strong dichotomy between indoors and outdoors. It is Christmastime, and characters make repeated references to the cold outside (a point that is emphasized visually for us by the heavy outer garments worn by the characters when they enter). The room, however, is warm and isolated; there is a stove, to which Nora tends to retreat whenever she is upset and which stands across the room from a window, showing the cold, dark world outside. There are also no less than three doors through which Nora must pass to make her final exit, the door she slams being the last one. The physical setting, then, emphasizes the safe, cozy world in which Nora has lived, in contrast to the harsh, cold world to which she will escape.

Question 4: How do the characterizations relate to those we have seen in Ibsen's previous plays? One starts, of course, with Nora. The students usually note that her characterization, for all its vivid realism, is of a type they have seen before: she is a Peer Gynt, a liar, a trickster, a spendthrift (note especially the little incident at the beginning where she overtips the delivery boy). She is also childlike (we even see her play with her children, as if she were one of them) and utterly amoral, yet personally devoted to her family, like Peer Gynt with his mother. The animal imagery associated with her, as she is called a lark, a squirrel, a dove, and so on, also echoes *Peer Gynt*, which abounds in animal imagery. Like Peer Gynt, Nora is in Kierkegaardian terms an "aesthetic" character, while her husband Torvald, by contrast, seems to be Kierkegaard's "ethical" man: a high principled, even priggish man who sets duty above the needs of family. If Nora is a realistic, bourgeois version of Peer Gynt, then Torvald is a realistic, bourgeois version of Brand.

In fact, each of the other characters in *A Doll House* tend also to be one of these two types. The villainous Krogstad turns out to be much like Nora, an amoral manipulator, devoted to his family. He even makes the comparison himself in act 2; when Nora begs him to consider her children, he replies, "Did you or your husband ever think of mine?" Conversely, Mrs. Linde and Dr. Rank, both moralists who constantly lecture Nora about duty and society, as does Torvald, are clearly of the ethical type. Ibsen, like Shakespeare, tends to use "reflector" characters, whose attributes parallel those of the main characters. Mrs. Linde, in particular, provides a model for what Nora is to become—independent, yet devoted to duty.

The line of discussion here is valuable because it helps students to understand the play as more than a simple, realistic work. Indeed, the symbolism of the characters is more important than what they may reflect from real life. *A Doll House* is a poetic construct, not *une tranche de vie*.

Question 5: What is Nora escaping? Where is she going? The Kierkegaardian terminology introduced in the previous question leads nicely into this one. For Kierkegaard, the idea of a leap, a sudden existential choice to live at a higher level, accounts for the way in which individuals develop. Similarly, characters make sudden self-transformations in many of Ibsen's plays: Agnes, and later Ejnar, in *Brand*; Consul Bernick at the end of *Pillars of Society*; Rita and Allmers at the end of *Little Ejolf*. Krogstad's sudden moral conversion at the beginning of act 3 both foreshadows Nora's own later conversion and reflects the Kierkegaardian pattern of transformation. When she first appears, Mrs. Linde has already undergone such a transformation; in fact, she has changed so much that Nora does not even recognize her. Thus, both character types and their transformations are "reflectors" in the play. (I have elaborated the character types and transformations in detail in my book, *Patterns in Ibsen's Middle Plays*).

Whether one employs Kierkegaardian terminology or not, it is a good idea to get students to see Nora's leaving in symbolic as well as realistic terms, noting how this action is paralleled and contrasted by other actions in the play and how the meanings of the action are established and reinforced by the details around it. The class has already noted that the setting creates a strong dichotomy between inside and outside. That cold, severe world outside makes Nora's leaving ambiguous. Ibsen often wrote such endings; we do not know in *Ghosts*, for example, whether Mrs. Alving will give her son the morphine pills, and our uncertainty makes the final curtain all the more dramatic. In *A Doll House*, we do not know what will happen to Nora after she slams the door, after she arrives in that outside world where we have heard so much of cold and darkness, of debts and work, of illness and death. Will she survive, given her background? And what is she escaping from? Not male tyranny—her husband, like her father, always loved her, and she loved them. Note how her forgery, around which the play's action revolves, was done not for her own benefit, as might have occurred in a simpler play, but to save her dying father from anguish and to restore her darling husband to health. She has never been physically abused, or even prevented from getting what she wanted. She has had three children whom, like her husband and father, she also has loved. (Even today, when leaving one's husband is more or less acceptable, a woman walking out on her children, as in the film *Kramer vs. Kramer*, seems shocking.) The play is not really about her "escape" but about her self-transformation; she has lived a warm, protected, childlike existence, and now, at long last, she has decided to grow up. She is not just leaving her husband but also finding herself.

This last question, then, brings the class full circle, back to the feminist issues raised at the beginning. But instead of simple-minded, black-and-white feminism, the play raises great questions about women's liberation, and beyond that (as Ibsen himself once said) about human liberation. The complexity of human relations; the importance of inner, personal transformation as well as outer, social transformation; the true nature of human freedom; the question of what constitutes a valid life—these are what *A Doll House* is really about.

PARTICIPANTS IN SURVEY OF IBSEN INSTRUCTORS

The following scholars and teachers of Ibsen graciously took time from their work to participate in the survey of approaches to *A Doll House*. Their ideas and information were an invaluable contribution to the volume.

Thomas P. Adler, Purdue University; Helen L. Baldwin, Frostburg State College; Rosemarie K. Bank, University of Toledo; Alice N. Benston, University of Rochester; Sr. M. Teresa Brady, The College of White Plains of Pace University; George B. Bryan, University of Vermont; Margie Burns; Vivian Casper, Texas Woman's University; Gay Gibson Cima, Georgetown University; Sara Coulter, Towson State University; Rosemary Curb, Rollins College; Rachel Dalven, Ladycliff College; Richard F. Dietrich, University of South Florida; David Downs, Northwestern University; Trudy Drucker, Bergen Community College; Donald G. Eisen, Indiana University of Pennsylvania; Beverly Elliott, Peirce Junior College; Tom Erhard, New Mexico State University, Las Cruces; Kenneth J. Ericksen, Linfield College; Rolf Fjelde, Pratt Institute; Verna Foster, Loyola University of Chicago; Krin Gabbard, State University of New York, Stony Brook; Mimi R. Gladstein, University of Texas, El Paso; Peter H. Greenfield, Whitman College; James W. Halporn, Indiana University; David W. Hart, University of Arkansas; Virginia Higginbotham, University of Texas, Austin; Donna L. Hoffmeister, University of Pittsburgh; Richard Hornby, Florida State University; Brian Johnston, Beirut University College; Joanne Gray Kashdan, Golden West College; Erna Kelly, University of California, Los Angeles; Susan Kelso, University of Kansas; Karen Laughlin, Florida State University; Arthur Lindley, National University of Singapore; John Lingard, University of Western Ontario; G. M. Loney, Brooklyn College; Sverre Lyngstad, New Jersey Institute of Technology; William B. Martin, Tarleton State University; Phyllis Mael, Pasadena City College; Cary M. Mazer, University of Pennsylvania; James Walter McFarlane, University of East Anglia; Lois More Overbeck, Agnes Scott College; Anthony Paré, McGill University; Bernard J. Paris, University of Florida; Robert Potter, University of California, Santa Barbara;

Otto Reinert, University of Washington; Richard C. Reynolds, Lamar University; Harry M. Ritchie, University of Denver; Katharine M. Rogers, Brooklyn College; Marvin Rosenberg, University of California, Berkeley; Pat M. Ryan, University of Trondheim; Paul Sawyer, Bradley University; June Schlueter, Lafayette College; Thelma J. Shinn, Arizona State University; Frances Shirley, Wheaton College; Rodney Simard, California State College, Bakersfield; Kathleen M. Skubikowski, University of Vermont; Nadine S. St. Louis, University of Wisconsin, Eau Claire; J. L. Styan, Northwestern University; Roland Torstensson, Gustavus Adolphus College; Karl Toepfer, University of California, Los Angeles; Robert Tracy, University of California, Berkeley; Carla Waal, University of Missouri, Columbia; Betty S. Waterhouse, Pennsylvania State University; Barbara D. Winder, Western Connecticut State University; Ute Winston, College of William and Mary; Barry Witham, University of Washington

WORKS CITED

Books and Articles

Abcarian, Richard, and Marvin Klotz, eds. *Literature: The Human Experience*. 3rd ed. New York: St. Martin's, ·1982.

Abrams, M. H. *Natural Supernaturalism: Tradition and Revolution in Romantic Literature*. New York: Norton, 1971.

Adelman, Irving, and Rita Dworkin, eds. *Modern Drama: A Checklist of Critical Literature on Twentieth Century Plays*. Metuchen: Scarecrow, 1967.

Aiken, Henry D., ed. *The Age of Ideology*. New York: NAL, 1956.

Althusser, Louis. *Lenin and Philosophy*. Trans. Ben Brewster. New York: Monthly Review, 1972.

Andersen, Annette. "Ibsen in America." *Scandinavian Studies and Notes* 14 (1937): 65–109, 115–46.

Archer, William. *Play-Making: A Manual of Craftsmanship*. London: Chapman, 1912.

———, trans. *The Works of Henrik Ibsen*. 12 vols. 1890. New York: Scribner's 1911.

Arestad, Sverre. "Ibsen in America, 1936–1946." *Scandinavian Studies* 24 (1952): 93–110.

Arvon, Henri. *Marxist Esthetics*. Trans. Helen R. Lane. Ithaca: Cornell UP, 1973.

August, Eugene R. " 'Modern Men'; or, Men's Studies in the '80's." *College English* 44 (1982): 583–97.

Barnet, Sylan. *A Short Guide to Writing about Literature*. 4th ed. Boston: Little, 1979.

Barranger, Milly S., ed. "Ibsen Bibliography 1957–1967." *Scandinavian Studies* 41 (1969): 243–58.

Barton, Lucy. *Historic Costume for the Stage*. Boston: Baker, 1961.

Baruch, Elaine Hoffman. "Ibsen's *Doll House*: A Myth for Our Time." *Yale Review* 69 (1979–80): 374–87.

Beckerman, Bernard. "Dramatic Analysis and Literary Interpretation: *The Cherry Orchard* as Exemplum." *New Literary History* 2 (1971): 391–406.

Bentley, Eric, "Ibsen: Pro and Con." 1950. *In Search of Theatre*. New York: Vintage, 1959. 344–56.

———. *The Playwright as Thinker*. New York: Harcourt, 1946.

Beyer, Edvard. *Ibsen: The Man and His Work*. Trans. Marie Wells. London: Souvenir, 1978.

Bien, Horst. *Henrik Ibsens Realismus*. Berlin: Ruetten, 1970.

Boleslavski, Richard. *Acting: The First Six Lessons*. New York: Theatre Arts, 1933.

129

Bradbrook, Muriel C. *Ibsen, the Norwegian: A Revaluation*. 1946. Hamden: Archon, 1966.

Brandes, Georg. *Henrik Ibsen, Björnsterne Bjornson: Critical Studies*. 1899. New York: Blom, 1964.

———. *Hovedstrømminger i det 19de Aarhundredes Literatur*. 1872.

Breed, Paul F., and Florence M. Sniderman, eds. *Dramatic Criticism Index*. Detroit: Gale, 1972.

Brockett, Oscar G. *History of the Theatre*. 3rd ed. Boston: Allyn, 1977.

Brustein, Robert. "The Crack in the Chimney: Reflections on Contemporary American Playwriting." *Theater* 9 (1978): 21–29.

———. *The Theatre of Revolt*. Boston: Atlantic-Little, 1962.

Bull, Francis. *Ibsen: The Man and the Dramatist*. London: Oxford UP, 1954.

Chekhov, Anton. *Notebooks*. Richmond: Hogarth, 1921.

Christensen, Erik M. "En meningsanalyse av Henrik Ibsens *Et dukkehjem*." *Hemeneutikk og litteratur*. Ed. Atle Kittang and Asbjørn Aarseth. Oslo: Universitetsforlaget, 1979. 121–35.

Clurman, Harold. *Ibsen*. New York: Macmillan, 1977.

———. "Interview with Harold Clurman by Yvonne Shafer." *Ibsen News and Comment* 1 (1980): 1–13.

Dietrich, Richard F. "Nora's Change of Dress: Weigand Revisited." *Theatre Annual* 36 (1981): 20–40.

Downs, Brian W. *Ibsen: The Intellectual Background*. Cambridge: Cambridge UP, 1946.

———. *Modern Norwegian Literature*. Cambridge: Cambridge UP, 1966.

———. *A Study of Six Plays by Ibsen*. Cambridge: Cambridge UP, 1950.

Dukore, Bernard F. *Money and Politics in Ibsen, Shaw, and Brecht*. Columbia: U of Missouri P, 1978.

Durbach, Errol, ed. *Ibsen and the Theatre: The Dramatist in Production*. New York: New York UP, 1980.

Eagleton, Terry. *Criticism and Ideology*. London: Verso, 1978.

———. *Marxism and Literary Criticism*. Berkeley: U of California P, 1976.

Egan, Michael, ed. *Ibsen: The Critical Heritage*. London: Routledge, 1972.

Ewbank, Inga-Stina. "Ibsen's Dramatic Language as a Link between His 'Realism' and His 'Symbolism.'" *Contemporary Approaches to Ibsen*. Ed. Daniel Haakonsen. Oslo: Universitesforlaget, 1966. 96–123.

Fergusson, Francis. *The Idea of a Theatre*. Garden City: Doubleday, 1949.

———. "Interview with Francis Fergusson by Rolf Fjelde." *Ibsen News and Comment* 4 (1983): 1–22.

Firkins, Ina Ten Eyck. *Henrik Ibsen: A Bibliography of Criticism and Bibliography*. New York: Wilson, 1921.

Fjelde, Rolf, ed. *Ibsen: A Collection of Critical Essays*. Englewood Cliffs: Prentice, 1965.

————, trans. *Ibsen: The Complete Major Prose Plays*. New York: Farrar, 1978.

————, trans. *Ibsen: Four Major Plays*. 2 vols. New York: NAL, 1965.

————, trans. *Peer Gynt*. By Henrik Ibsen. Minneapolis: U of Minnesota P, 1980.

Flores, Angel, ed. *Ibsen*. New York: Critics Group, 1937.

Ganz, Arthur. "Miracle and Vine Leaves: An Ibsen Play Rewrought." *PMLA* 94 (1979): 9–21.

Gassner, John. *Masters of the Modern Drama*. 3rd rev. ed. New York: Dover, 1954.

Gay, Peter. *The Education of the Senses*. Vol. 1 of *The Bourgeois Experience*. New York: Oxford UP, 1984.

Gilman, Richard. *The Making of Modern Drama*. New York: Farrar, 1974.

Gosse, Edmund. *Henrik Ibsen*. New York: Scribner's, 1910.

Gray, Ronald. *Ibsen: A Dissenting View*. Cambridge: Cambridge UP, 1977.

Guerin, Wilfred L., et al. *A Handbook of Critical Approaches to Literature*. New York: Harper, 1966.

Haakonsen, Daniel. *Henrik Ibsen, mennesket og kunstneren*. Oslo: Aschehoug, 1981.

————. "Tarantella-motivet i *Et dukkehjem*." *Edda* 48 (1948): 263–75. Rpt. in Paul, *Ibsen*. 197–211.

Hardwick, Elizabeth. *Seduction and Betrayal*. New York: Random, 1975.

Haugen, Einar. "Ibsen in America." *Journal of English and Germanic Philology* 33 (1934): 396–420.

————. *Ibsen's Drama: Author to Audience*. Minneapolis: U of Minnesota P, 1979.

————. *Norwegian-English Dictionary*. 3rd ed. Oslo: Universitetsforlaget, 1984.

Haugen, Einar, and Kenneth G. Chapman. *Spoken Norwegian*. 3rd ed. New York: Holt, 1982.

Hegel, Georg Wilhelm Friedrich. *Hegel: Texts and Commentary*. Trans. and ed. Walter Kaufman. Garden City: Doubleday, 1966.

Heiberg, Hans. *Ibsen: A Portrait of the Artist*. London: Allen, 1969.

Heistrüvers, Hans-Dieter. "Bild und Rolle der Frau in unserer patriarchalischen Gesellschaft, behandelt am Beispiel einer soziologischen Interpretation von Ibsens Schauspiel *Nora oder Ein Puppenheim*." *Der Deutschunterricht* 24 (1972): 94–118.

Heller, Otto. *Henrik Ibsen: Plays and Problems*. Boston: Houghton, 1912.

Holtan, Orley I. *Mythic Patterns in Ibsen's Last Plays*. Minneapolis: U of Minnesota P, 1970.

Hornby, Richard. *Patterns in Ibsen's Middle Plays*. Lewisburg: Bucknell UP, 1981.

————. *Script into Performance: A Structuralist View of Play Production*. Austin: U of Texas P, 1977.

Høst, Else, "Nora." *Edda* 46 (1946): 13–28. Rpt. in Paul, *Ibsen* 180–96.

Hurt, James. *Catiline's Dream*. Urbana: U of Illinois P, 1972.

Ibsen, Bergliot B. *The Three Ibsens*. London: Hutchison, 1951.

Ibsen, Henrik. "Et dukkehjem." *Nutidsdramaer 1877–99*. Oslo: Gyldendal; København: Jorgensen, 1962. 67–114.

————. *From Ibsen's Workshop: Notes, Scenarios, and Drafts of the Modern Plays.* Trans. A. G. Chater. Ed. William Archer. 1911. New York: Da Capo, 1978.

————. *Samlede Vaerker.* 20 vols. København: Gyldendalke Boghandels, 1898.

————. *Samlede Verker.* Ed. Didruk Arup Seip. 3 vols. Oslo: Gyldendal, 1960.

Jaeger, Henrik. *Henrik Ibsen, 1828–1888, A Critical Bibliography.* Trans. William Morton Payne. 2nd ed. Chicago: McClurg, 1901.

Jameson, Fredric. *The Political Unconscious: Narrative as a Socially Symbolic Act.* Ithaca: Cornell UP, 1981.

Jameson, Storm. *Modern Drama in Europe.* New York: Harcourt, 1920.

Johnston, Brian. *The Ibsen Cycle.* Boston: Twayne, 1975.

————. *To the Third Empire.* Minneapolis: U of Minnesota P, 1980.

Jorgenson, Theodore. *Henrik Ibsen: A Study in Art and Personality.* Northfield: St. Olaf College P, 1945.

Kashdan, Joanne G. "A Doll House." "Ghosts." "Hedda Gabler." "Peer Gynt." "Rosmersholm." *Masterplots.* Ed. Frank N. Magill. Rev. ed. 12 vols. Englewood Cliffs: Salem, 1976.

Kennedy, X. J., ed. *Literature: An Introduction to Fiction, Poetry, and Drama.* 2nd ed. New York: Little, 1979.

Kerans, James. "Kindermord and Will in *Little Ejolf.*" *Modern Drama: Essays in Criticism.* Ed. Travis Bogard and William I. Oliver. New York: Oxford UP, 1965. 192–208.

Kernan, Alvin. *Character and Conflict: An Introduction to Drama.* 2nd ed. New York: Harcourt, 1969.

Kierkegaard, Søren. *Either/Or.* Trans. David F. Swensen and Lillian Marvin Swensen. 2 vols. Garden City: Doubleday, 1959.

Knight, G. Wilson. *Henrik Ibsen.* New York: Grove, 1962.

Koht, Halvdan. *Life of Ibsen.* Trans. and ed. Einar Haugen and A. E. Santaniello. New York: Blom, 1971.

Kott, Jan. "Interview with Jan Kott by Yvonne Shafer." *Ibsen News and Comment* 1 (1980): 6–7.

Krutch, Joseph Wood. *"Modernism" in Modern Drama: A Definition and an Estimate.* Ithaca: Cornell UP, 1953.

Landy, Alice S., ed. *The Heath Introduction to Literature.* 2nd ed. Lexington: Heath, 1984.

Lavrin, Janko. *Ibsen: An Approach.* New York: Russell, 1950.

————. *Ibsen and His Creation: A Psycho-Critical Study.* New York: Haskell, 1972.

Le Gallienne, Eva. "Acting in Ibsen: An Interview with Eva Le Gallienne by Yvonne Shafer." *Ibsen News and Comment* 2 (1981): 1–16.

————, trans. *Eight Plays by Henrik Ibsen.* Rev. ed. New York: Random, 1982.

————. "Ibsen, the Shy Giant." *Saturday Review* 54 (1971): 23–26.

————, trans. *Six Plays by Henrik Ibsen.* New York: Modern Library, 1957.

Lessing, Doris. "To Room Nineteen." *Literature: The Human Experience.* Ed. Richard Abcarian and Marvin Klotz. 3rd ed. New York: St. Martin's, 1982. 567–90.

Lester, Elenore. "Ibsen's Unliberated Heroines." *Scandinavian Review* 66 (1978): 58–66.

Lucas, F. L. *The Drama of Ibsen and Strindberg.* New York: Macmillan, 1962.

Luce, Claire Booth. *A Doll's House 1970 (with Apologies to Henrik Ibsen). Images of Women in Literature.* Ed. Mary Anne Ferguson. Boston: Houghton, 1973. 358–69.

Lyons, Charles R. *Henrik Ibsen: The Divided Consciousness.* Carbondale: Southern Illinois UP, 1972.

Marker, Frederick, and Lise-Lone Marker. "The First Nora: Notes on the World Premiere of *A Doll's House." Contemporary Approaches to Ibsen.* Ed. Daniel Haakonson. Oslo: Universitetsforlaget, 1971. 84–100.

Matthews, Brander, ed. *Papers on Playmaking.* New York: Hill, 1957.

McFarlane, James Walter, ed. *Discussions of Henrik Ibsen.* Boston: Heath, 1962.

———. *Henrik Ibsen: A Critical Anthology.* Harmondsworth: Penguin, 1970.

———. *Ibsen and the Temper of Norwegian Literature.* New York: Octagon, 1979.

———, trans. and ed. *The Oxford Ibsen.* 8 vols. London: Oxford UP, 1960–77.

McFarlane, James Walter, and Jens Arup, trans. *Four Major Plays.* By Henrik Ibsen. London: Oxford UP, 1982.

Mencken, H. L. Introduction. *Eleven Plays of Henrik Ibsen.* 1917. New York: Random, n.d.

Meyer, Hans George. *Henrik Ibsen.* Trans. Helen Sebba. New York: Ungar, 1972.

Meyer, Michael, trans. *Brand.* By Henrik Ibsen. Garden City: Doubleday, 1960.

———, ed. and trans. Ghosts *and the Three Other Plays.* By Henrik Ibsen. Garden City: Doubleday, 1962.

———. *Ibsen: A Biography.* Garden City: Doubleday, 1971.

———. *Ibsen: Plays: Two,* 2 vols. 1965. London: Methuen, 1980.

Noreng, Harald. "Et dukkehjem." *Henrik Ibsen: Norske og utenlandske foredrag under Minneuken 1956.* Oslo: Aschehoug, 1956. 106–19.

Northam, John. *Ibsen: A Critical Study.* Cambridge: Cambridge UP, 1973.

———.*Ibsen's Dramatic Method.* London: Faber, 1953.

———. "Ibsen's Search for the Hero." *Edda* 60 (1960): 101–20. Rpt. in Fjelde, *Ibsen: A Collection.* 91–108.

Østvedt, Einar. *"Et dukkehjem": Forspillet, skuespillet, etterspillet.* Skien: Rasmussen, 1976.

Palmer, Helen H., ed. *European Drama Criticism 1900–1975.* Hamden: Shoe String, 1977.

Paul, Fritz, ed. *Henrik Ibsen.* Darmstadt: Wissenschaftliche Buchgesellschaft, 1979.

Reinert, Otto, and Peter Arnott, eds. *Thirteen Plays.* Boston: Little, 1978.

———. *Twenty-Three Plays.* Boston: Little, 1978.

Richter, Jean Paul, ed. *The Notebooks of Leonardo da Vinci*. 2 vols. New York: Dover, 1970.

Rieger, Gerd Enno. "Noras Rolenengagement." *Orbis litterarum* 32 (1977): 50–73.

Robins, Elizabeth. *Ibsen and the Actress*. 1928. New York: Haskell, 1973.

Rogers, Katharine M. "A Woman Appreciates Ibsen." *Centennial Review* 18 (1974): 91–108.

Rosenberg, Marvin. "Ibsen vs. Ibsen or: Two Versions of *A Doll's House*." *Modern Drama* 12 (1969): 187–96.

Sharp, R. Farquharson, trans. *Four Great Plays by Ibsen*. New York: Bantam, 1959.

Shaw, George Bernard. *Our Theatres in the Nineties*. 3 vols. London: Dodd, 1937.

———. *The Quintessence of Ibsenism*. New York: Hill, 1964.

Sprinchorn, Evert. "Ibsen and the Actors." *Ibsen and the Theatre: The Dramatist in Production*. Ed. Errol Durbach. New York: New York UP, 1980. 118–30.

———, ed. *The Genius of the Scandinavian Theatre*. New York: NAL, 1964.

———, ed. *Ibsen: Letters and Speeches*. New York: Hill, 1964.

Stanislavski, Constantin. *An Actor Prepares*. Trans. Elizabeth Reynolds Hapgood. New York: Theatre Arts, 1936.

———. *Building a Character*. Trans. Elizabeth Reynolds Hapgood. New York: Theatre Arts, 1949.

———. *Creating a Role*. Trans. Elizabeth Reynolds Hapgood. New York: Theatre Arts, 1961.

Stanton, Stephen S., ed. *Camille and Other Plays*. New York: Hill, 1964.

Strømberg, Ulla, and Jytte Wiingaard, eds. *Den levende Ibsen: Analyser af udvalgte Ibsen-forestillinger 1973–78*. København: Borgen, 1978.

Stuart, Donald Clive. *The Development of Dramatic Art*. 1928. New York: Dover, 1960.

Tennant, Peter. *Ibsen's Dramatic Technique*. Cambridge: Bowes, 1948.

Valency, Maurice. *The Flower and the Castle: An Introduction to Modern Drama*. New York: Macmillan, 1963.

Van Laan, Thomas. *The Idiom of Drama*. Ithaca: Cornell UP, 1970.

Watts, Peter, trans. *A Doll's House and Other Plays*. By Henrik Ibsen. New York: Penguin, 1965.

Weigand, Hermann J. *The Modern Ibsen: A Reconsideration*. 1925. New York: Dutton, 1960.

Williams, Raymond. *Marxism and Literature*. Oxford: Oxford UP, 1977.

Williams, Simon. "The Well-Made Play." *The Romantic Century*. New York: Scribner's, forthcoming.

Wisenthal, J. L., ed. *Shaw and Ibsen: Bernard Shaw's* The Quintessence of Ibsenism *and Related Writings*. Toronto: U of Toronto P, 1979.

Zucker, Adolf Eduard. *Ibsen: The Master Builder*. New York: Holt, 1929.

Films

A Doll's House. Narr. Norris Houghton. Encyclopaedia Britannica, 1967.

————. Dir. Patrick Garland. With Claire Bloom and Donald Madden. 1973.

————. Dir. Joseph Losey. With Jane Fonda and David Warner. World Film Series, 1973.

Edvard Munch. Dir. Peter Walkin. ITC Entertainment, 1971.

First Monday in October. Dir. Ronald Neame. With Walter Matthau and Jill Clayburgh. 1981.

Hedda Gabler. BBC–Time-Life, 1976.

Kramer vs. Kramer. Dir. Robert Benton. With Meryl Streep and Dustin Hoffman. 1980.

The Wild Duck. BBC–Time-Life, 1976.

Recording

A Doll's House. Dir. Hilliard Elkins. With Claire Bloom and Donald Madden. Caedmon, TRS, 1971.

INDEX

Tennant, Peter, 26
Tiblin, Mariann, 23

Valency, Maurice, 27, 46, 95, 108
Van Laan, Thomas, xiv–xv, 26

Warner, David, 41
Watts, Peter, 4
Weber, T., 8
Wedekind, Franz, 33, 74

Weigand, Hermann J., 28, 39, 48, 52, 61, 87
Wiingaard, Jytte, 26
Wilder, Thornton, xii
Williams, Raymond, 76, 86–87
Williams, Simon, 26
Williams, Tennessee, 42–43
Wisenthal, J. L., 27
Witham, Barry, 31

Zucker, Adolf E., 27, 52